ALSO BY D. W. BROGAN

THE ENGLISH PEOPLE
Impressions and Observations

"Mr. Brogan has with rare understanding and good humor delineated the Englishman of caricature and of reality. And he has delineated him for the edification of Americans, and in an idiom that Americans will understand and welcome. There is probably no one else who could have done this job quite as well. . . ."
—Henry Steele Commager in
New York Herald Tribune Weekly Book Review

PUBLISHED BY ALFRED A. KNOPF

The American Character

THE

American

Character

BY

D. W. Brogan

NEW YORK · ALFRED A. KNOPF · 1944

THIS BOOK HAS BEEN PRODUCED
IN FULL COMPLIANCE
WITH ALL GOVERNMENT REGULATIONS
FOR THE CONSERVATION OF PAPER, METAL,
AND OTHER ESSENTIAL MATERIALS

TO

NELL BURNETT

Contents

Preface

THIS BOOK is ambitious in design but modest in its actual detail.
It is designed to make more intelligible to the British public certain
American principles and attitudes. But it makes no pretense to either
profundity or elaborate learning. A great many important aspects of
American life have been ignored or treated very sketchily, sometimes
because they were irrelevant to my immediate object, sometimes because I thought myself incompetent to handle them.

I have been writing on American topics for fifteen years. Inevi-
tably I have sometimes repeated myself. I have not tried to find novel
ways of saying the same thing. "The American Way in War" appeared in part in *Harper's Magazine*.

As readers will soon discover, this is a personal book. I have made
assertions because I thought them to be true and relevant, not because they had a weight of independent authority behind them.
There may result from this plan of work an air of impertinence and
casualness. But nothing could be further from my intentions or attitude than to treat any serious American topic frivolously. My object
has been to make what I think is the most interesting country in the
world interesting and intelligible to others. Above all, I have tried to
make plain that there is no parallel in history to the experiment of
free government on this scale. The scale accounts for a great deal,
including the apparent justification at some periods and in some departments of American life for pessimism about the present or the
future of America. In the past, the pessimists have always been wrong.
I think they are still wrong.

D. W. BROGAN

London, March 24th, 1944.

Introduction

IN THE LATE SUMMER of 1936, I arrived in Kansas City (Missouri). When I tried to buy a ticket for St. Louis at the Union Station, I was interrogated in a friendly, American fashion by the ticket clerk. "You from Europe?" "Yes." "Well, don't go back—it's going to Hell." I was more than half-convinced that he was right—although I was going back. A month or so before, I had lain on the shore in Somerset on a Sunday evening and had been aroused from day-dreaming by a noise in the air and a swirl of excitement around me. Above, magnificent, serene, and ominous was a Zeppelin, moving east. It was low and clearly seen; a day before, it had been in New York; by tomorrow's dawn it would be in Frankfort. The swastika was plainly visible as it moved on, over Glastonbury where, the legend runs, Joseph of Arimathea had brought the Holy Thorn and built the first Christian church in Britain. A shadow was crossing England: women on the beach looked at their children—with a faint and how inadequate perception of what was soon to befall Bristol where they came from. How remote it all seemed in the hot sun of western Missouri, how remote it was even from me, and how much more remote from the people of Midwest America, with fifteen hundred miles each way between them and the oceans, with the huge war memorial outside the station to remind the citizens of Kansas City of their first adventure overseas and to confirm their resolution that it would be the last.

I went a day or two later to see a friend of mine who lives in a small town in Illinois. We went together to the corner drugstore to get ice cream for supper. It was a scene familiar enough to me and familiar to all movie-goers—the Main Street of a small American town on a Saturday night in late summer. The boys and girls were there in their white summer clothes; there were endless cars; it was possible that here, as in other American towns like this, it was thought more important to have a car which is a public asset than a bathroom which is private. There was over the street and over the town that indefinable American air of happiness and ease, at least for the young. There was that general friendliness and candor. Here, as much as in the Bowery of which he was the Boss, men and women were acting on the principle laid down by Big Tim Sullivan, "God and the People hate a chesty man."

People called each other by their "given names"; there were friendly inquiries and a few introductions of the visitor. It was a world in which the ominous word "stranger" had been given a friendly flavor. "Howdy, Stranger" is not a hostile greeting, and it was invented in America. Looking at the people, at the boys and girls milling round the drugstores, disappearing in cars that shot off into the warm, welcoming darkness, it was hard to remember the tension of English life, the worse tension of French life. Life, it is true, was not altogether easy and agreeable for these people. Those who had definitely put youth behind them showed signs of fatigue and worry. They had reason. This was a farm town and the farmers had had a bad time. Some, not very far away, were still having a bad time. Across the Missouri it was a drought year. In Emporia, Kansas, it was still doubtful, so William Allen White had told me, whether they could reopen the local normal college that Fall. There might not be enough water. All that region had been badly hit by very bad times, by crop failures, by bank failures. But there was still an impression of hope, of recovery. There was an air of confident adaptation to their way of life in the dress, the speech, the manners of the young. This, if a world they had not made, was yet a world that seemed to have been made for them.

In the drugstore there was the usual stock of gadgets, of remedies for all ills. There were soft drinks, no hard liquor; but there was—most impressive sight of all—a book and magazine section. There were the books of the films; there was the book of the year or decade (it was the first year of *Gone with the Wind*). If you wanted to know about dressmaking, about cosmetics, about domestic management, about love, about astrology, about business success, about child training, about how to be happy on a small income (the answer being usually a way to make it large), the printed oracles were there. And the spoken oracles, too, for radios blasted the soft summer night and the heat did not empty the movie house.

And it was all American—even the guiding stars. The advertisements, the gadgets, the radio programs, the movies, the patent medicines, the patent solutions to human woes—all were American, or almost all. There might be in the advertising sections some sales talk for English biscuits or French perfume or Scotch whisky. There might be in the movie house a travelogue by Fitzpatrick; there might be in the St. Louis *Post-Dispatch* a cartoon by a greater Fitzpatrick bringing home the bitter truth about the outer world. No doubt some residents in the town had traveled (my host had). Perhaps the librarian or the English teacher had told the women's club of a tour in England or the "colorful Caribbean." Some veterans had memories of France.

The regional press was already doing a first-class job, a better job than was being done by most English papers, to awaken the people to the truth of the new iron age that we were all living in, to the significance of Manchukuo, to the menace of international war in Spain. Perhaps, the Parent-Teachers' Association had asked for more instruction in civics and in current affairs. Certainly, appeals for charity, for Chinese, or for Spaniards had been or would be answered as soon as made.

But in the warmth and ease of that summer night, the inevitable, the right, the human character of American natural isolationism was brought home to me. The road from Jerusalem to Jericho did not pass close to southern Illinois, as it did southern England, and there was no visible good Samaritan in Illinois—or in England—to shame Priest or Levite.

Their great highway was the Mississippi; for its control a long and bloody war had been fought and won. From that state had come the leader of the victorious party, but Lincoln was long dead and deified in his tomb a hundred or so miles to the north in Springfield. The whole region had once been a great international prize, but it was a century and a half since George Rogers Clark had seized the little French settlements of Kaskaskia and the rest from the English. It was over a century, too, since his brother William and Meriwether Lewis had marched west at the orders of President Jefferson, making for the Pacific, preparing the road maps of "manifest destiny." It was a generation since Henry Adams had brought his sophistication and his bile to the St. Louis Exposition and thought out again the problem of what makes and moves and unites societies, what was alike and unlike in Chartres in 1200 and in St. Louis in 1904—"the Virgin and the Dynamo." But in 1936, it was the calm, dead center of a tornado whose outer boundaries were too far away for comprehension or apprehension.

There was no way in which the inevitable, deplorable, maddening impact of the outside world on Illinois and on the whole Mississippi Valley could be brought home to the dwellers therein. If men and women in England in 1938 could profess to believe in "peace in our time," why should not these happy Americans believe with far more plausibility in peace in their time—for them? Yet in less than six years, German submarines were sinking American ships in the mouth of that Mississippi secured for the infant United States through the energetic disregard of constitutional proprieties by President Jefferson. And all the considerable cities of the Valley were preparing to defend themselves against air raids, against desperate, forlorn hopes in which the Nazis would strike, whatever the cost, at the most typical, representative, important city of the Midwest—which naturally was Zenith or whatever city was yours.

As the shadow over Europe grew longer and darker, as the darkness was made more terrifying by the whistling with which our leaders tried to keep up their courage and ours, as the chances of peace in Europe became more and more dependent on the temptations of easy victory for Germany, and those temptations more and more controlled by the possible reaction of the American people, the problem of the American temper became more urgent. It was largely a question of time: if the American people had been prepared in 1931 to do what they were prepared to do in 1939, if they had been as ready in 1939 as they were in 1941 for the dangers of the time! But it is an endless sequence of ifs that it is not very profitable to follow out. What is more profitable is to try to make plain how natural, how justifiable, how given by historical conditions was the tempo of American awakening, the slow acceptance of the fact that the shadow cast over Somerset was also cast over Illinois. It took the actual shadow, repeated again and again, to awaken Somerset; Illinois had to awaken with far less help from the eye and ear.

But it was not only Illinois. All over the United States there was the same life, conditioned by the same history, by an experience in which the outside world grew more and more remote, backward, barbarous, and—so it was thought—relatively weak. On the new concrete roads, new-model cars made American nomadism the expression of American civilization. "God's Country"—as the song put it—was the country of the Lincoln Highway. Into the great inland nodal points the trains poured: Illinois Central; New York Central; Union Pacific; Chicago, Milwaukee & St. Paul; Père Marquette; Atchison, Topeka & Santa Fe. But only a few Canadian trains in the north, only a few Mexican trains in the south, to recall the outside world, and doing it not much more effectually than an occasional Rolls-Royce or Duesenberg or Hispano-Suiza lost among the Lincolns, Packards, Buicks, Chevrolets, Fords. The air was getting fuller of passenger planes; the air ports more numerous and more splendid. And it was as natural, though as wrong, to think of the new technique as an American invention and practically an American monopoly, as to think of Colonel Lindbergh as the first man to fly the Atlantic.

What could it mean to the remote villages of the South, to the people who worshipped in those little wooden churches with their odd, pathetic, and fantastically ugly imitations of stained glass? Did it matter to them that the French had put an aerodrome beside Chartres Cathedral, and that the latest addition to the inscriptions at that place was an appeal for volunteers to join the organization that would move the Chartres stained glass to a safe place when the inevitable war (that no one would admit or deny was coming) yet came? This region had had its war, its record of destruction; and its wounds, material and spiritual, were still bleeding.

Yet that region, in five years' time, was beginning to send its volunteers via Canada, to fight in defense of that Wells Cathedral over which the Zeppelin had serenely passed.

What could it matter to the *Canadiens* of New England? What did it matter to them that the country that had expelled the *Acadiens* and conquered the *Canadiens* was in danger and, with it, the ancestral land that had abandoned the good ways of old France and no longer had enough sons to guard her fields? In less than six years' time the New England coast was beleaguered by submarines, and their kinsmen from across the border were dying first at Dieppe and then in a heroic assault outside Ortona.

What did it matter to the less energetic fugitives from a New York winter I saw a few months later, who, resisting any temptation to take a ski train up to the White Mountains, took a train bound for Florida? Yet inside five years, the submarines of the enemy were cruising in impudent immunity within rifle shot of the pleasure cities where the tourists lay on the sand, or profited and lost in Colonel Bradley's hospitable gambling houses.

I remembered, too, the long controversy over bridging San Francisco Bay, the doubts of the War and Navy Departments about the wisdom of building such vulnerable structures across the entrance to a great naval base. Such fears had seemed purely fantastic, purely pedantic. Yet within three years of the celebration of the completion of the bridges, the dead and wounded from Pearl Harbor were being brought ashore in San Francisco. And, a few months later, I stood in the living-room of a friend's house looking straight into the Golden Gate and wondering, like other people, how the great naval battle of the Coral Sea was going and whether the Japanese would risk putting a carrier or two into the permanent summer fog belt and bomb San Francisco as they had bombed Pearl Harbor. I remembered, too, how I had first seen Seattle, taken over by invading Lions or Elks or Moose or Eagles, and how I had next seen it, with a solitary barrage balloon (from London) floating over the air port, curiously homely and comforting to a passenger who had just seen the great ice fields and glaciers of Mount Rainier below him and had need of something to restore a human sense of scale.

Our fate, the fate of civilization in Europe, the fate of constitutional freedom in America are and were bound up with the defeat of a self-confident, energetic, efficient, and ruthless political and military system that denies our premises and dislikes and despises our aims. This was true in 1936; it is true in 1944. It was the meaning of the shadow cast over England. But that shadow was not cast in such dramatic form over America.

What could this growing shadow mean to the people of Utah? It was nearly a century since the members of the Church of Jesus Christ of Latter-Day Saints had crossed the prairies and the plains to the great empty basin of the Great Salt Lake. Nearly a century had passed since they had made their Exodus, since they had been saved from the crickets by the seagulls sent by God to preserve his chosen people. I had seen the monument to the seagull; I had seen the irrigated fields and fertile valleys redeemed from the wilderness; I had heard the hymn of the new Israel, the Mormon version of the Hundred and Fifth Psalm: "Unto thee will I give the land of Canaan, the lot of your inheritance." The old bloody feuds, the murder of the Prophet, the vengeance of the Destroying Angels, were half forgotten by the people who sang "Come, come, ye Saints." Isolated in the great, empty basin, shut in by mountains on all sides, living in the land they had made; with their own, exclusive version of world history to cut them off from the fears and hopes of the outside world, what could Hitler mean to them? Yet in a few years' time, not merely were their sons sent to all corners of the world, but the needs of war economy were transforming Deseret as it had not been transformed since the railroads brought in Gentiles to the kingdom of Brigham Young.

What, I more than once reflected, could all this mean to the shepherds of New Mexico who elected Dennis Chavez of Los Chavez ("Chavez of that ilk," as they would say in Scotland) to the United States Senate? "The blood of the conquerors," to use Harvey Fergusson's phrase, no doubt ran in their veins; so did the blood of the conquered. But that last outpost of New Spain had been for long so peaceful! The Comanches had been tamed, and the bloody memory of the seventeenth-century Indian rising that had for twelve years turned the little capital of Santa Fe into a heathen town, was faint, today. The austere and bare mountains of the Sangre de Cristo above the stripling Rio Grande del Norte were as strange as ever to European eyes, as strange as they must have been to Miss Willa Cather's hero when the future Archbishop came to them a century ago, from the strange but not arid, not empty mountains of Auvergne. Peace had at last come to Santa Fe and to Taos. But in less than six years from that summer, there fell on the little cities and villages of New Mexico the catastrophe, the heroic disaster of Bataan. For the local National Guard had been mobilized and sent off to the Philippines, and boys who had known nothing of the outer world died in gallant defense of another relic of the Christian empire of Philip II and Philip III—the Commonwealth of the Philippines, reunited with New Mexico in a common destiny by the power of the United States.

And that power was so easy to underestimate, and each such underestimation made war more likely. It was easy for the Japanese to underestimate it; for, as Mr. Justice Black had pointed out, the Japanese, like the Americans, believe that they have never lost a war. It had been easy to surprise the somnolent Tsarist Russians at Port Arthur in 1904; it would be easy to surprise the complacent, ill-informed, and unsuspecting Americans at Pearl Harbor in 1941—to "catch them with their pants down," in the expressive American phrase; and one of the Japanese diplomats negotiating in Washington while the trap was being got ready prided himself on his command of American idiom.

It was easy for the Germans to despise the people whom Herr von Papen in 1916 had described as "those idiotic Yankees." True, the idiotic Yankees had been too much for Herr von Papen and his employers, but that was in the bad old days. I remembered a discussion in Paris in 1939 with a very eminent White Russian diplomat, a Baltic baron by origin, who told me that his friends in the German Embassy were not in the least interested in the power of the United States. "Whatever they do will be done too late. And if that warmonger Roosevelt does try to impede the policy of the Reich, there will be a revolution against him and his Jewish advisers." So spoke the experts of the Third Reich. I said that I did not believe this; that

I knew America well, that to awaken the national pride and anger of the American people would be the most fatal mistake of the gamblers in charge of the destiny of Germany and the peace of Europe. I even told the revealing story of what had happened to John Quincy Adams in 1797 when he was sent by his father, President John Adams, as Minister to Berlin. "When the American Minister to Prussia, the son of the President, arrived at the capital of Prussia, he was examined by a dapper young officer of the guard, who unblushingly admitted that he had never even heard of the United States of America." * A century and a quarter later, a successor of John Adams and John Quincy Adams in the White House deposed the Hohenzollerns, and another quarter of a century after that, another successor was Commander-in-Chief of an army which put more men in the air over Berlin than Washington had Americans under him at Valley Forge or at Yorktown.

I remembered, too, that when the British troops under General O'Hara marched out at Yorktown in 1781 to surrender to Washington and Rochambeau, their bands played *The World Turned Upside Down*. And as in the darkening months and years, I heard the apologists for the new Danegeld preach the policy of buying Hitler off—even, if absolutely necessary, with British property—I wondered whether they, with their subservience to the new enemy of all American political religion, really cared nothing for American goodwill or whether, like the Germans, they thought that it was a mere matter of sentiment, that there was time enough before the American giant awoke to see that he should awake, like Gulliver in Lilliput, bound hand and foot.

But many of them, English and German, did not even think that he was a giant, that the world had really been turned upside down at Yorktown, that it was time for even the smuggest Prussian expert or English politician to learn what it meant that the United States had grown to its present stature and to its present unity.

That the Japanese and Germans made a mistake they are now learning the hard way. That those of us who underrated the speed and power of American action were wrong, we are now learning in a much more agreeable fashion. Yet the American problem remains.

* Bennett Champ Clark: *John Quincy Adams*, p. 61.

It is a double problem. It is the problem of making intelligible to the American people the nature of the changes in the modern world which they can lead, or which they can resist, but which they can't ignore. That is a problem for Americans. There is the second problem: the problem of making intelligible the normal American's view of the world, of his own history and destiny. Full success in the solution of such a problem is impossible; there must always remain an element of the unconscious and unintelligible in the national life of any people. But a little can be done to encourage sympathetic understanding of the Americanism of America.

The problem of modern America is almost literally one of orientation. A century ago, Henry Thoreau described how, when he went out of doors uncertain where to go, his instinct always decided for him. "I turn round and round irresolute sometimes for a quarter of an hour, until I decide, for the thousandth time, that I will walk into the southwest or west. Eastward I go only by force; but westward I go free. Thither no business leads me. It is hard for me to believe that I shall find fair landscapes or sufficient wildness and freedom behind the eastern horizon. I am not excited by the prospect of a walk thither; but I believe that the forest which I see in the western horizon stretches uninterruptedly toward the setting sun, and there are no towns or cities in it of enough consequence to disturb me. Let me live where I will, on this side is the city, on that the wilderness, and ever I am leaving the city more and more and withdrawing into the wilderness. I should not lay so much stress on this fact if I did not believe that something like this is the prevailing tendency of my countrymen. I must walk toward Oregon and not toward Europe." *

All American experience, down to very recent times, was on the side of Thoreau. Oregon was no longer the wilderness; the Columbia River no longer rolled hearing "no sound save its own dashings," but was tamed by the greatest dams in the world and—towards the ocean, at least—rimmed with cities. But the westward drive was still potent; Americans rejoiced still in "the inward eye which is the bliss of solitude." It is only in this century that they have begun to learn, slowly, inadequately, humanly, that the world is really round, that to walk toward Oregon is to walk toward Europe. It has been a shock to their

* Quoted by Bernard De Voto: *The Year of Decision 1846,* "Invocation."

optimism, a shock to their view of their destiny. It is now necessary to turn from the lesson of Thoreau—or to apply it in a new world. Honolulu is west of Oregon; China, "the Orient," is west of Honolulu; the Aleutians and Siberia are north and west. A contemporary of Thoreau knew that mere movement in one direction is not a solution.

"Were this world an endless plain, and by sailing eastward we could for ever reach new distances, and discover sights more sweet and strange than any Cyclades or Islands of King Solomon, then there were promise in the voyage. But in pursuit of those far mysteries we dream of, or in tormented chase of that demon phantom that, some time or other, swims before all human hearts; while chasing such over this round globe, they either lead us on in barren mazes or midway leave us whelmed." *

The world is round, and so you come to Europe (or Europe comes to you) by the back if not by the front door. The world runs north and south as well as east and west. Brazil is a neighbor of Africa as well as of the United States; Canada is a neighbor of Siberia as well as of Greenland.

And it is not only a world that has closed in on the United States (or on whose once remote borders the United States now presses with unconscious weight and power). It is a world in which all nations have to make deep adjustments in their mental habits, have to take stock of what is living and what is dead in their traditions. But that adjustment must, all the same, be made in the terms of the living tradition, according to the spirit. "These are the times that try men's souls," wrote Thomas Paine in 1776. These are the times that try men's powers of sympathetic imagination, of mutual understanding, for without these there will be no enduring structure of peace and order built.

* Melville: *Moby Dick*, Chapter LII.

The American Character

PART ONE

America Is Made

*"East were the
Dead kings and the remembered sepulchres:
West was the grass."*
—ARCHIBALD MACLEISH

IT IS NEARLY four hundred and fifty years since white men began to settle in North America, and three hundred and fifty years since the first unsuccessful settlements of English-speaking people were founded. The settlement of North America, the filling-up of its vast empty spaces, is the most remarkable extension of one society over an ocean barrier of which we have any knowledge. Century after century, tens of millions of Europeans have crossed three thousand miles of ocean, leaving behind them an old, reasonably adapted society in a familiar and, on the whole, friendly physical environment. They have brought with them European ideas, European techniques, European bodies and physical habits. They have brought these to an empty continent and it has taken them centuries not merely to fill that continent, but to create ways of life adapted to a different climate, to a different set of economic possibilities, and to a society held together at its beginnings by imported political and social habits, and only slowly and with repeated crises creating American political and social habits to replace the European importations that, with each decade, wore thinner and thinner like an old carpet. In this process the modern American has been created; the interplay of geographic, biological, historical forces has made him. And the process has seemed reasonably complete only in our own time. Only in this century has the continental territory of the United States been formally organized into uniform political units; only in this century has the centuries-old ambition of the extension of the area of settlement westward and further westward turned from a possibility to a nostalgic dream; only in this generation has the practical cessation of large-scale immigration ensured that nearly all the young people of the United States should be American-born, instead of being diluted by a million new Europeans arriving every year to be adjusted, often very inadequately, to the necessary conditions of American life.

The historical process that has in this century produced so American an American society was long, difficult, and novel. The first settlers in what is now the United States were confronted with forest all along the line from Maine to Florida. Before them lay over a million square miles of "the forest primeval, the murmuring pines and the hemlocks," forest on a scale that Europe had not known for two thousand years. Scattered over that forest were a few hundred thousand natives, Indians. They were limited in their possibilities of adaptation by the comparative poverty of their natural environment and by their incapacity to alter that environment. They had no horses, no cattle; they had to be hunters and planters, and it was impossible to build a populous and progressive society in the forest on these terms. It was not a matter of native incapacity. The Indian took to the horse and the gun with great speed; some of the European techniques he accepted quickly, and others he might have accepted if the invaders had given him time to do so. But the adjustment of the Indian to his environment, often admirable though it was, was not an adjustment that the white man wanted to make or could make. Before an American society could be created by the settlers, America had to be transformed. The forest had to give way to the fields, the plow, the draft ox, the mule, the sheep, the goat, the wheel, gunpowder, steel had to make possible a new life in which tens of millions could live abundantly where a few hundred thousand savages had been living precarious and poverty-stricken lives. America had to be made before

it could be lived in, and that making took centuries, took extraordinary energies and bred an attitude to life that is peculiarly American. It bred the temper of the pioneer, the temper of the gambler, the
temper of the booster, the temper of the discounter of the future who
is to some extent bound to be a disparager of the past. It took optimism
to cross the Atlantic, optimism or despair and anger at the old world
from which the reluctant pioneer had come. Until this century, there
was always tempting the adventurous or the unlucky the dream of
a new chance a little farther on. Movement became a virtue, stability
a rather contemptible attitude of mind. The frontier in English speech
is a defined barrier between two organized states; in American it is a
vague, broad, fluctuating region on one side of which is a stable, settled, comparatively old society, and on the other, empty land, a few
savages, unknown opportunities, unknown risks. American history has
been a matter of eliminating that debatable area between the empty
land and the settled land, between the desert and the sown. This
elimination has now been completed, but it is too early, yet, for the
centuries-old habits to have changed and much too early for the attitude of mind bred by this incessant social process to have lost its
power. Bishop Berkeley was a premature prophet when in the eighteenth century he wrote:

> *Westward the course of empire takes its way,*
> *The first four acts already past.*
> *The fifth shall close the drama with the day,*
> *Time's noblest offspring is the last.*

The fifth act is with us, but neither the actors nor the spectators
yet know its issue or know whether it will have a tragic or a happy
ending.

When the early settlers from crowded Europe saw the more fertile
parts of the Atlantic coast, empty, promising, asking for the plow
and the herd, it was natural that they should underestimate the difficulties of settlement. It was natural that speculators in Europe should
see themselves, for the expenditure of a little capital, suddenly shot
upwards in the social scale. Land was abundant in America, scarce
in Europe; owning land was socially and financially the aim of all

climbing Europeans in the seventeenth century—and it was a climbing century. The new western lands seemed to offer promotion for everybody, for great magnates who wanted even more, for the cadets of noble houses who in Virginia need not be the victims of primogeniture, needy younger sons, but could quickly set up in the New World as equals of their elder brothers. Even when the dreams of gold and silver were found to be baseless, there was still the land. And for the first two centuries of English settlement, it must always be remembered, the astonishing mineral resources of what is now the United States were unreachable. Gold and silver there was in abundance—but undiscovered in what was then Spanish territory. Other metals, iron and copper; other minerals, soft coal and anthracite; oil and natural gas; the repeated bonuses Nature paid to the Americans in the nineteenth century were withheld from the first settlers. And because this was so, the dream of an easy ascent to gentility without labor was a dream that never came true. The role of the mere proprietor, the mere owner of naked legal titles to land, was never an easy one. To make money out of land in America, you had to work and watch; a mere gentry living off rents could not be and never was created. The American equivalent of the English squire was never a close equivalent; he had to be a gambler, an entrepreneur, a capitalist; he had to be vigilant, generation after generation, to keep his old land from deterioration and to secure his share of the new land. If he did neither, he could not keep up with the Joneses who on the frontier were repeating the pattern of the first settlement. From the very beginning, American life was competitive from the top downward. There was no real stability, no real security for anyone. Here and there a family might stay put; here and there mere stability paid well enough. But such cases were few, and fewer still the fortunes, the social and political positions, preserved over centuries without repeated effort, without setbacks and windfalls. There was no high plateau of effortless superiority to be attained, by Byrds in Virginia or by Saltonstalls in Massachusetts. A family or an individual had to have what it took to survive—and it took adaptability, toughness, perhaps a not too sensitive moral or social outlook. The would-be profit-drawers in England simply contributed capital on which no return was or could be made. The would-be gentry unlearned the idle lessons of gentility or sank into poverty or returned to the easier world they had left. From the beginning it was "root, hog, or die." And the American razor-back hog that the forest bred, with little meat and much muscle, was a symbol as well as a product of the process of adaptation.

The poor who came to America—the majority of the settlers—had fewer illusions to shed than had the gentry. They took a rationally pessimistic view of the world and did not expect to get anything for nothing. Whether they were solvent enough to pay their way (the mere cost of transportation was relatively very high indeed in these days), or sold themselves as indentured servants to earn, by seven years' serfdom, the passage to America, or were transported, free, by a vigilant government for offenses ranging from taking the wrong side in a rebellion to plain and fancy felonies, the move to America was important and final. They did not expect to go back; if they were religious or political refugees they did not want to. And the new world into which they came had to be made habitable by them.

Adaptation again was the key. How many early settlements—Spanish, English, French—withered away or were swept away by famine and disease! To pick the wrong, malarial, snake-infested, swampy site for the settlement, that was a mistake paid for by the loss of the meager capital resources so painfully accumulated—and often by the forfeit of life as well. To fail to plant the right crops at the right time was a mistake as deadly. The early settlers of New England bore in their memories the duty of gratitude to the Indians who taught them the completely novel technique of planting Indian corn (maize), the making of the little mound like a golf-tee, the use of fish as a fertilizer—ways so new to wheat-growers, to users of plows and breeders of cattle. The timing of your arrival on the American coast (as much a matter of good luck as of good navigation) might mean death for all or most of a party before the first crops could be harvested.

The early settler had to have an eye for the country, he had to be a real estate dealer, to make a good first choice, to decide whether it was wiser to hold on, whether it was wiser to cut your losses, to file that petition in bankruptcy which moving on constituted, whether it was possible to unload your losses on some more optimistic and more gullible newcomer. Again, there were some exceptions. The Germans who settled in early Pennsylvania have stayed put ever since, and their fertile, well-formed, stable countryside often evokes nostalgia in European breasts. But America was not made by ways of life that evoke European nostalgia or by imitations of European stability, and the "Pennsylvania Dutch" have played a far less important role than those more American-type immigrants, the so-called "Scotch-Irish," the Ulster Presbyterians who took into the Indian country whisky, Calvinism, a high degree of pugnacity, and a taste for acquisition on a big scale.

In the first century, geographical stability was suggested if not imposed by the lie of the land and the balance of power. In harbors and up rivers were the natural centers of settlement. Great mistakes were made; "obvious" sites like New York were for a time neglected, hopeless sites like a score of decayed or abandoned old settlements were chosen. But with the sea behind them and the numerous rivers opening ways inland, the early settlers were distributed, very thinly, all along the coast in a fashion fairly obviously dictated by geography. The sea still bound them to Europe, to an England which was from a transportation point of view easier of access from Charleston (South Carolina) than was Boston (Massachusetts) from the same port. The umbilical cord that bound the new, unadapted settlements to the mother country ran up the great rivers, too. Where ships could go, un-American forces were still holding the settlers to the old world and to old ways. The West might beckon—the American sees the sun move from the ocean inland; his evening view over the Atlantic is gray and grim, while "to the west the land is bright." But where falls and rapids broke the easy navigation channels, the "Fall Line" of the geographers limited settlement. Beyond that, it was no question of ships out of London or Bristol, but of that admirably functional invention of the Indian, the canoe, and in winter that other Indian invention, the snow-shoe. (Only in the last few years has the American adopted the even more functional Norwegian ski for winter use, for cattle-tending as well as for winter sports.)

Along the coast, clearing the forest was comparatively easy; communication between settlement and settlement, between colony and mother country, comparatively easy too. But away from the coastal plain, it was very different. The only easy river way into the heart of America was in French hands, so the masters of the St. Lawrence were exploring the Mississippi and seeing the possibilities of what is now the site of Chicago, while the English settlers were still pinned to the coast. True, there runs inland from New York the admirable natural road of the valleys of the Hudson and the Mohawk. But across this corridor lay the most formidable of Indian warriors, the Five Nations of the Iroquois. They were allies of the English against the French; they co-operated with the first great Irish-American politician, Colonel Thomas Dongan, Governor of New York for James II. But they were a barrier that the feeble colonists could not then force.

And far more feeble tribes than the Iroquois were barriers too. In the early days the Indians were not outnumbered. As they got guns from the quarreling European settlers, they were not hopelessly outclassed in equipment, and the forest, hundreds of thousands of square miles of it, was their home. To it they were adapted; to its climate, its trails, its honey, its cranberries, its game, to its possibilities for the hunter and warrior. The English settler had to learn all this; perhaps no settler really learned the necessary woodcraft—but his sons did. An Indian war in the seventeenth century was no joke. To push too far inland was to risk disaster and the holding up of westward advance for a generation. This was learned on the Connecticut River round Northampton, more recently famous as the home of cautious Cal Coolidge and of one of the most famous of American women's colleges, Smith. Monuments, tradition, a local patriotism that is genuine if carefully cultivated, keep this memory green among the Polish and Italian children of the region today. It was a far more vivid and compelling memory a century ago, and a positive barrier to reckless advance two centuries ago. When the whole frontier flamed up in one of the recurrent wars with France, fortunate and few were those, from Maine to the Carolinas, who lost neither life nor scalps nor cattle nor friends. Eternal vigilance was the price not of liberty only but of life; the early settlers long needed to acquire a craft equaling the craft of the savages and a savagery not much inferior.

It is hard to remember this today in a pleasant village like Farmington, even with the sparsely settled communities of Maine not far north of Boston to remind us how American America was. But it has to be remembered all the same.

If the settlers on the Atlantic coast had to adjust themselves to a new world, how much more the settlers in the late eighteenth century who passed the mountain barrier and entered the Mississippi Valley! On the seaboard the ocean route to England was still open. The planter, the merchant, the minister, the physician could order books and clothes and luxuries from the old world; he could and did dream of a visit "home," could sigh like Increase Mather after the metropolitan delights of Newington Green, could recall in tranquillity like Franklin the courts he had seen and the king he had dined with. Across the mountains, it was a far newer world. All the great valley was veined with creeks and streams and rivers—all finding their way to the Mississippi and the Gulf of Mexico. Once in the Valley, geography conspired to unite all the Valley dwellers one with another and to cut them off from the seaboard and from Europe. Many hundreds of miles away lay the Spanish King's city of New Orleans that one Bourbon monarch had transferred to another just as the English-speaking tide began to lip over the mountains. To that remote trading town, the rivers drew the settlers. For them there was no importation of English broadcloth and Spanish wine. They had to fend for themselves, make their own crude tools and their own rough textiles, ship east their one valuable small-bulk product, whisky, and their bulk products, corn and hogs and hides, down the rivers to New Orleans. Down river was easy enough, but up river was slow, dangerous, and unprofitably laborious. The men and women who went into the West were necessarily stripped to bare necessities by their environment.

The primitive life of those stranded pioneers, belated survivals of the eighteenth century, the mountaineers of Tennessee and the Ozarks, shows what was involved in settling the Great Valley. Men and women came into it with capital laboriously brought from Europe or laboriously accumulated on the seaboard. And that capital was sunk in opening the West. The children of the settlers were more American than their parents, better adjusted to their environment, with less of the luxuries of the old world about them. They read less— if they could read; they had fewer books, fewer refinements; their equipment of English and Scottish ballads, their Bibles, their *Pilgrim's Progress* and Blackstone's *Commentaries* represented diminishing assets. In the seaboard settlements, it had been possible to create, on a basis of tobacco and rice raised by slave labor in the South, of slave trading, of careful commerce in rum and molasses and cod and ships in the North, a reasonably plausible simulacrum of the contemporary civilized society of England. Boston and Philadelphia, Charleston and the great Virginia plantations were not in the least barbarous communities, though their wealth, their culture, and their social structure were more adequate than ample. The Virginia plantation houses were elegant, at any rate when they were first built, but by the standards of English magnates they were small and cheap. Even Westover was far from being a Woburn or a Chatsworth. The little cities were clean and often in parts elegant; Charleston was beautiful. But they were small and provincial compared not only with London, but with the Edinburgh of Principal Robertson, the Glasgow of Professor Adam Smith, the Birmingham of Joseph Priestley and James Watt. They were outposts of the old world rather than capitals of the new.

Far more American and far more touching to the historical imagination are the old towns of the Middle West. They are not old by American standards, much less by European; some of them—St. Louis and Cincinnati, for instance—have become great cities like other great American cities. It is not the cities that made the grade which are touching and symbolic, but the little towns that did not. Vincennes, Marietta, Bardstown, Lexington—these were centers of civilization, of learning, of religion, of commerce. Some, like Gallipolis, represent highly unsuccessful enterprises; others had their brief day and now are content to be minor centers, like Cairo. Here was an early college; there an early cathedral. This town had the first steamboat in its region; that one sank all its capital in a now grass-grown canal. And all around these little settlements was the forest or the ominous empty meadows of Kentucky's "dark and bloody ground." All around them were the Indians; the southern kinsmen of the Iroquois; new tribes like the Choctaw and the Cherokee. New names replaced old Indian names. Pontiac and Tecumseh played the roles of Powhatan and King Philip. There were wars and massacres. Chicago remembers the massacre of Fort Dearborn; all the West remembers Tippecanoe and Fallen Timbers; knows who opened Ohio, who Alabama, for whom Jackson and Fort Wayne are named. That typical Middle-Western

town, Muncie, Indiana—the city made famous as "Middletown"—
gets its name from an Indian tribe whose chief Little Turtle gave his
daughter in marriage to the white adventurer who opened up the
region as Powhatan had given Pocahontas to John Rolfe. The place
names show the intermingling of races and cultures in the vast forest
land. Indian names are everywhere: Ohio and Tennessee, the Wabash and the Scioto; Chicago and Sheboygan. There are French
names—Vincennes and Jawbone that was once Narbonne. There is
St. Louis named under Louis XV to commemorate Louis IX, and
Louisville that was called after Louis XVI, as Marietta is called after
Marie Antoinette. There is Terre Haute in Indiana and its Hellen-
ized version, Akron, in Ohio. There is Lexington that commemorates
the first battle of the Revolution, and Washington and Jefferson,
Madison and Franklin, are commemorated over and over again.
There are Springfields that recall New England, and "licks" like
French Lick that tell us that here the necessary salt was found. There
is Memphis as well as Cairo, Salem and Warsaw. Ypsilanti recalls the
Greek War of Independence; there is Toledo and New Madrid;
Racine and Oxford. It is a palimpsest with one line hastily written
over another as the whites moved in like so many imitators of Adam,
naming rivers and lakes, hills and towns in the land they had to
conquer and create.

For even more than on the seaboard, the forest was here an enemy.
So it was attacked as an enemy; devastated like the Palatinate by the
French or Munster by the English. It was burned; forest fires were
the most natural thing in the world with the newcomers pressing on.
The great trees were girdled, their bark cut through till they died;
their stumps were left in the ground; the pioneer farmer plowed or
planted round them. The rifle and the ax were at least as necessary as
the spade or the plow. Many of the first settlers were semi-nomads
like Lincoln's father, fonder of hunting and fishing than of the steady
toil of the peasant; ready to move on when the deer and the fish, the
bears and game birds grew scarcer or the half-stripped land either
salable or obviously worthless. These men were illiterate, often
drunken, often violent. They had lost a great deal in their adaptation
to the Indian world of the forest. They resented, sometimes, the book-
learning coveted by boys like the young Lincoln; they would have

appreciated better a son like Huckleberry Finn. They might have become as completely assimilated to the Indian way of life as did so many of the French *coureurs de bois* like the great Du Lhut, after whom the great iron port of Duluth is named. But they were saved from that by their numbers and by their women. To live like the Indians meant to live thinly, scattered over the forest, paying respect (except in wartime) to the hunting rights of neighboring tribes, meeting on neutral grounds like Kentucky; a way of life that the world has delighted to read about since Cooper created the Indian legend, but which the modern world has refused to live. The men crossing the mountains from the English settlements were not a handful like the French coming into the Great Lakes from the St. Lawrence; they came in tens of thousands, year after year; they crowded out the Indians; they crowded out their own semi-nomad population. They were farmers, not fur traders or hunters; they were bad, wasteful, unsettled, technically backward farmers, but they were farmers all the same. And they did not come alone—the women came with them.

It was a hard world for the men; it was a far harder world for the women. For all the elements of a woman's life had to be created; the home had to be built, the settled community life had to be created; the possibility of a non-savage life for the children had to be made out of nothing. It was on the women, confined to the cabin, that the worst hardships fell. They died of plagues like the milk-sick; their children died of it. They died in childbed; if modern America seems full of widows, America a century ago was full of widowers. It was the women who suffered from the laxity of the marriage bond, from the footloose husband or lover, from the savage feuds bred in drinking bouts, from the shiftlessness of the man who could and did live much as does an animal, taking little permanent interest in his children or their mother. It was Lincoln's stepmother who encouraged him to read, who gave him his first glimpse of civilization. It was she to whom his gratitude went out; his father he despised and ignored. It was Lincoln's wife, from the comparatively old and well-settled state of Kentucky, who tried to make a tidy, socially ambitious man out of the frontier lawyer; she failed, but the second wife of her old beau and her husband's great rival, Stephen Douglas, was more successful. She made the Little Giant dress better and drink less. When Mark

Twain made Tom Sawyer's aunt undertake the civilizing of Huckleberry Finn, he may have had his own experience in mind, the adjustment of the manners of a Mississippi pilot to the social standards of Elmira or Hartford; but, whether he had or not, he created an effective symbol. The Mississippi Valley needed to have its hair combed, it needed to have someone see that its boys washed behind the ears.

It was the women who supported the missionaries who came into the wilderness to preach against drink and fornication, to preach for stable marriage, for the literacy needed to read the Bible, for those bourgeois virtues that the Middle West then needed so badly and is only now rich enough, settled enough, secure enough to begin to think it can despise. Great Methodist circuit riders like Peter Cartwright were makers of the society of the Great Valley. So in a less dramatic way were those less flamboyant pioneers like the "Yale Band" who tried to carry New England orthodoxy into a region that needed stronger meat. The revival meeting, orgiastic, anti-intellectual, often ludicrous, was as necessary to the organization of a stable society in the Middle West as the steamboat that could move upstream from New Orleans to St. Paul. Religion, if sufficiently emotional, simple, and relevant could move upstream, too, against the permanent temptations to savage anarchy that the frontier pressed on men who had a natural bias toward anarchy, toward adventure, or they would not have crossed the mountains into the untamed land.

And it was not only the preachers and the women who fought anarchy, who fought the temptations of savage life. The politicians did, the lawyers did. They were great figures in the West round 1800. Sometimes, like Andrew Jackson, they were soldiers and planters as well as politicians and judges. But the western leader who came to the top by his power of speech, of debate, by his energy and courage (he might have no other standard virtues) was a founder of commonwealths. The young Henry Clay, "the mill boy of the slashes," moving from Virginia to Kentucky and leading the "War Hawks" of 1812 who wanted war to punish the English—and weaken the Indians— was a maker as well as a product of the West. And his power was the power of speech, the power of law. So it was with less brilliant, less well remembered figures like Thomas Hart Benton, Jackson's leader in the Senate. So it was with that extraordinary figure, Sam Houston, adventurer, politician, soldier, who actually passed years living among the Cherokees with an Indian wife, ready for that unknown destiny that was to make him the hero of Texas—relying as he did, in old Roman fashion, on the favorable omen of an eagle. Clay, Benton, Houston, all had in common a devotion to the Union, to the political system that had made their careers possible, that had in two generations filled the Mississippi Valley from the Canadian border to the Gulf of Mexico with free commonwealths, linked together by the most sacred bond, the Constitution of the United States. That constitution worship that sometimes seems so odd today was not odd to them. It was the moral far more than the physical authority of the federal government that had held the infant union together in the critical years before President Jefferson bought Louisiana—i.e., the western bank of the Mississippi and the essential gate to the outer world, New Orleans—from Napoleon. It was Jefferson who had broken the conspiracy of Aaron Burr. It was Jackson who had given the toast, "Our federal union, it must be preserved." It should be remembered that it was quite easy for the settler in the Middle West to have no dealings at all with the government of the United States. He paid no direct taxes; he very often wrote no letters and received none, for the good reason that he and his friends could not write. Yet the only ubiquitous federal officials and federal service were the Postmasters and the Post Office. There were no soldiers except in the Indian country; there were federal courts doing comparatively little business. True, the new union had built the National Road, down which creaked the Conestoga wagons with their cargo of immigrants' chattels. It fought the Indians from time to time and it had at its disposal vast areas of public lands to be sold on easy terms and finally given away to settlers. But no government that had any claim to be a government at all has had less direct power over the people it ruled. Politics was bound, in these conditions, to be rhetorical, moralizing, emotionally diverting, either a form of sport or a form of religion. The political barbecue, the joint debates between great political leaders were secular equivalents of the camp meeting and the hell-fire sermon.

In the hard and often drab life of the slowly consolidating western society, politics, for the men at any rate, was a welcome diversion.

Torchlight processions, debates that sometimes ended in fights, violent press campaigns that sometimes ended in duels—these were welcome in the days before organized sport had undertaken to provide vicarious excitement for millions. But the role of politics was not always so divorced from drab economic reality. It was a fact of great importance that the West was developed with hardly any interference from the outside, that the necessary minimum of political organization was provided locally and spontaneously, that the West got as much law and order as it thought it needed—and its needs were not exorbitant. There was no organized police force; the local sheriff, totally dependent on local opinion for his posse, for his power of effective action, was no very good match for such organizations as the Murrell gang before the Civil War or the James Boys after it. But when disorder became intolerable, there was a new sheriff, or a lynching, or what in the Far West came to be called a Vigilante organization. As settlement grew closer, simple murder and banditry became more difficult and less tolerable. But the idea of the imposition of order from the outside, of an absolutely inflexible system of law enforced with cold impartiality, was not a western idea. A lawyer there needed to have more than his wits about him; he needed personal prestige—a reputation for honesty, courage, presence of mind, or accurate marksmanship, or for all of these qualities—before he could be a success as a defending counsel, not to speak of a district attorney or a judge. Effective law was an aspect of the character of some man or men.

Yet if there was a good deal of lawlessness, there was real respect for law. There was a general acceptance of the authority of the State and the Union. There was no equivalent of Spanish-American revolutions, no encouragement given to mere *pronunciamientos*, though a man like Andrew Jackson in a Spanish environment would have had all the talents and temperament and temptations of a dictator. But Jackson and his followers and enemies gave to the Constitution of the United States the reverence due to "the supreme law of the land." The federal government was forced to make adjustments in its too rigid land laws, to recognize the effective rights of squatters on the public lands. Locally, it was polite not to ask too many questions of a man arriving from another state, with or without a lady companion. But no society could have grown so fast if the minimum basis of law had not been provided by the free choice of the people, the only effective authority. On the western frontier, the general will, like the political equality of all (white) men was no fiction of a political philosopher but an observable reality.

The system was tested very severely indeed in California where, for the first time, the Americans had to deal with the problems of a society suddenly made rich by gold, not slowly made rich by work, a society in which there were few women, a society in which cities sprang into existence overnight without the long discipline of exploration, settlement, urban growth. Any human society might have been baffled by the problem of San Francisco in 1850—and some societies would have found better remedies for disorder than highly respectable organized lynch law. A few years later, British authority preserved legality and order far more effectively in Australia and in British Columbia than American authority did in California. But then among the things with which California had to contend was an invasion of "Sydney ducks" and other hard cases from the convict settlements of infant Australia, and no Californian looking at the results—Australia and California—will doubt which method bore the more delicious, superior, and colossal fruit. Yet even in California, the civilizing influences were soon at work as the story of the mother of the philosopher Josiah Royce shows. The first, masculine, anarchical barbarism was soon being assailed by women, by teachers, by politicians. California settled down—at any rate, as much as it was reasonable to expect of that favored land and exuberant population.

Few things, on consideration, prove less surprising than the evaporation of federal authority over the South once secession was adopted. Almost the only federal institution that meant anything to the common man was the Post Office—and by a statesmanlike turning of the blind eye, the new Southern Confederacy continued to allow the federal government to deliver the mail even after the seceding states had formally broken with the Union. What is surprising is not the disappearance of federal authority from Washington south to the Mexican border and west to Arizona, but the fact that, at a cost of half a million lives, it *was* restored in a four-year war that imposed on the North as great an ordeal as any victorious nation has undergone in modern times and on the South a defeat whose penalties in loss of life, wealth, and security were proportionately far greater than those imposed on Germany by the loss of the war of 1914-18.

The impact of the Civil War on American life and American memory can hardly be exaggerated. It is still "the war"; its heroes on both sides give their names to forts and training camps (Sheridan, Thomas): from its leaders, on both sides, tanks take their names (Grant, Sherman, Stuart). From 1868 (the first post-war election) to 1900 inclusive, every man elected President of the United States had with one exception been an officer in the Union army; all but one were ex-generals. Round it legend of all kinds clustered; it is still a sure-fire subject for fiction and the movies. Its battlefields and war cemeteries are sacred in an especial way. Chancellorsville, Fredericksburg, Vicksburg, Stone River, Chickamauga, Lookout Mountain, Atlanta, Petersburg—these are still fighting names. The tactics, the strategy of the war are fought over again in magazines, in reviews, in books. South of the Potomac it is still a near-fighting word to call this conflict anything but "the War Between the States." There are still unreconstructed rebels in Georgia and men who still think treason odious in Vermont—and northern Tennessee. The Civil War is not the only genuine American war (as apart from wars waged by the United States). There is the War of the Revolution, there is Bunker Hill and Brandywine. There is the War of 1812 with its memories of victories on sea to offset defeat on land—and the memory, too, of that crowning victory of New Orleans, won after peace had been made, a victory cherished for its very pointlessness—and for giving in Jackson Day (January 8th) a national festival to the Democratic party. There are Indian wars, too; in Minnesota, perhaps the Sioux War of 1862 is as important as the share of the new state in the Civil War. And in Texas, the war against Mexico is the center of state and world history. But all of these wars are American wars, fought on American soil about issues local to America, relevant to the great theme of the conquest and use of the American soil. In the First World War more American lives were lost than in any domestic war except that of 1861-65; but it was not merely an undertaker's ramp when the bodies of the American dead were brought back to America. There was no American equivalent of Rupert Brooke's conviction that his body would make "some corner of a foreign field . . . forever England," no monument in the Argonne or at Cantigny that has anything like the hold on American hearts and memories that Vimy Ridge has for Canadians or the beaches of Gallipoli for Australians and New Zealanders. No war fought outside the present boundaries of the United States has so far been taken to the hearts and memories of the American people. The Marines may commemorate "the halls of Montezuma" and "the shores of Tripoli," but for the average American, the really sacred sites are places like Concord where the first shots of the Revolution were fired against the British or Gettysburg where Lee's army,

> *broken, reeled*
> *From a stubborn Meade and a barren field.*

And Concord and Gettysburg have this other claim to memory that their ideological meaning was made plain by two utterances that have become American classics. At Concord, said Emerson:

> *By the rude bridge that arched the flood,*
> *Their flag to April's breeze unfurled,*
> *Here once the embattled farmers stood*
> *And fired the shot heard round the world.*

And that shot echoed eighty-eight years later in Lincoln's declaration that "We here highly resolve that these dead shall not have died in vain—that this nation, under God, shall have a new birth of freedom—and that government of the people, by the people, for the people, shall not perish from the earth."

It has long been fashionable to reduce the ideological content of the War of the Revolution and the Civil War to, at most, a trace. But even if the "glittering generalities" of the Declaration of Independence, like their echo in the Gettysburg speech, will not stand strict semantic or historical examination (which is not yet proven), the fact that the American people believe that their two great ordeals by battle, in one of which the new nation was born and in the other saved, had their origin in different views of the political good life is a fact of great practical importance. It puts a limit to the possibilities of mere *Realpolitik* as a possible American policy. To ignore this is not to be realist but to be romantic.

Nevertheless, the emotional interest evoked by the Civil War has other roots, too. For what was at issue was not solely the moral character of slavery (though that was at issue), nor the rights and duties of minorities (though that was at issue), nor the nature of the federal union (though that was at issue). It was the unity, the future of the great interior valley in which alone the character of a new American people could be given to the immigrants, from Europe and from the Atlantic seaboard alike. The decisive event of those years was the entry of the railroad into the Mississippi Valley, an event even more decisive than Nicholas Roosevelt's first Mississippi steamboat. For the steamboat only made it easier to exploit the river system; the railroad made it possible to defy it. No longer must traffic run north and south, with such successful though not decisive modifications as the Erie Canal that joined the Great Lakes to the mouth of the Hudson and made New York the unquestioned metropolis, or such failures at modification as that Potomac Canal in which George Washington saw the solution of the old problem of joining Virginia to the West. The railroads defied the map. They went west across the mountains or, when New York got round to it and found its canal monopoly threatened, by the flat road Nature had provided up the Hudson and across by the Mohawk. They linked the Mississippi Valley to the seaboard as it had never yet been linked. The Union was made real by the new iron bonds that each year got farther west—to Albany, to Pittsburgh, to Wheeling, to Columbus, to St. Louis, to Chattanooga, to Atlanta, to Chicago, to St. Joseph. But these bonds were bonds binding the West to the North. Only Chattanooga and Atlanta were southern versions of the great American novelty, the town whose basic position was created by the railroad, such as Chicago and Kansas City and Omaha. No longer did the rivers tie up the Great Valley to New Orleans; the railroads tied it up to New York and Philadelphia and Baltimore. The battle for the control of the new West, economically, politically, socially, was won by the side that had the most railroads; the war in a double sense was a railroad war; it was fought to upset an old economic and political balance of power, and the war that arose from this attempt was won by the side that the railroads fought for. It was symbolic and more than merely symbolic that the only really important case in which Lincoln was ever briefed was a railroad case; that his rival, Stephen Douglas, was a great railroad lawyer and spokesman; that President Jefferson Davis of the Southern Confederacy had, as federal Secretary of War, tried to secure that the transcontinental railroad, when it came, should take the southern route.

Within five years of the end of the war, the great representative river port, St. Louis, at the junction of the Missouri and Mississippi, had built its magnificent Eads bridge over the levees at which the river steamers were beginning to be tied up to rot. And it was no accident that within five years of the ending of the war, the English-speaking tide that had slowly crept from the Atlantic to the Missouri in two hundred and fifty years had rushed over the fifteen-hundred-mile gap to California.

With the coming of the railroad, some victories over the American land were made possible that no energy, courage, or ingenuity could have won before. The settlers, habituated to the great forest, had reluctantly and with much trepidation ventured forth on to the lone prairie. Indeed, it was English settlers, more used to open country, who in Illinois had dared to leave the well-watered and wooded river bottoms for the great sea of grass. On the open prairie there was no timber for housing to build the log cabins of the pioneers, to provide timber for the rails that Lincoln, like so many more, had split to make fences, no timber for fuel, and little water that had not to be dug for. But with the coming of the railroad came corrugated iron and wire fencing and commercial timber for houses, and young trees to make windbreaks, and traveling salesmen from which the farmer could order new-fangled gadgets like windmills and reapers, and his wife could order new-fangled gadgets like sewing machines. The railway that brought could take away; the once practically self-supporting farmer was now forced to sell his grain at world prices, fixed in Liverpool and relayed (with modifications) through the Chicago Board of Trade, the "Pit." He had always been a gambler; now he was more of a gambler than ever, a gambler with little knowledge but with great courage. But the land was fertile. Europe was growing richer and more greedy. To the west lay the High Plains where the buffalo roamed in millions till the railroad cut the great herd in two, till the Winchesters of tourists and buffalo-hide hunters and cattlemen eager for grazing lands reduced the bison to a few thousand guarded specimens on reservations where the Indians, deprived of their whole economic basis, had preceded him. It was no wonder that to the outside world, the typical western hero of this generation should be called "Buffalo Bill."

For a few years, the open range reproduced the life of the nomad Indian with the semi-savage Texas Longhorns and the not very civilized cowboys as representatives of the buffalo and the Indian. Those were the days when the great American legend of the Wild West was created for the delight of the whole white world. Then the great western bandits and bad men replaced the Gargantuan figures of Mississippi legend like Mike Fink, the giant boatman, or the Finn McCool or Little John of the northern forest, Paul Bunyan. Mike Fink and Paul Bunyan were legends; not so the James Brothers or the Dalton Brothers or such precocious bad men as Billy the Kid or the most remarkable killer of them all, the boy John Wesley Hardin. Again, settlement had gone much faster than order. The new frontier was lawless enough. Cheyenne, Dodge City, Tombstone with its Boot Hill cemetery for those deceased residents who had died with their boots on—these were reflections on the American sense of order.

So, too, were the Indian wars which the experience of Canada showed could have been avoided and which produced the apparently ludicrous spectacle of two great soldiers like Sherman and Sheridan who, a few years before, had commanded armies of scores of thousands, directing the movements of little columns pursuing such masters of American war and politics as Chief Joseph, Geronimo, and Sitting Bull. And there was irony as well as tragedy in the fact that in the year in which the centenary of American independence was celebrated, the Sioux under Rain-in-the-Face destroyed the dramatic and dramatized General Custer and all his men at the Indian Cannae, the Little Big Horn, where the mounted savages rode round and round the doomed whites like Hannibal's Numidian cavalry and—more fortunate than the Carthaginians—left their own pictographic record of their victory. But no savage generalship could defeat civilization. On the plains of Texas, the six-shooter made the white man on a horse more than a match for the mounted Indian with his bow and arrow who had hitherto been more than a match for a man armed only with a single-shot rifle. The Winchester repeating rifle did the job farther north, and more and more railroad lines cut across the prairie and the High Plains. Sheepmen came into the cow country and fought for the possession of the strategic water holes without which it was useless to have legal title to tens of thousands of acres. New mining camps like Leadville repeated in Colorado the violent history of California. The open range over which cattle moved a thousand miles from Texas to Canada began to be cut up into ranches, wired off and guarded. Big cattlemen fought open and concealed wars with little cattlemen, using force when chicane failed. The bitter winter of 1886 ruined big and little alike—and put an end to the easy profits of the Edinburgh land companies which had revived in Scottish breasts the seventeenth-century hopes of easy profits to be drawn across the Atlantic. New state after new state was added; the last free Indians were herded into reservations; vigilant and quick-shooting sheriffs like Bat Masterson provided a reasonable amount of law and order; and by the centenary of the Constitution (1889) the West was no longer, by western standards, wild. It was served and ruled by the great railroads whose names are as magical to Americans, almost, as the names of the great rivers that the railroads robbed of so much economic importance: Union Pacific, Southern Pacific, Texas Pacific, Northern Pacific, Great Northern, and that line which, in its very title, sums up the history of the American movement into the country of the Indian and the Spaniard—the Atchison, Topeka & Santa Fe.

In 1890, a hundred years after the four million settlers on the Atlantic seaboard were first numbered, the federal census took note that the frontier was closed, and a poet in one deservedly immortal couplet summed it all up:

Across the plains where once there roamed the Indian and the Scout,
The Swede with alcoholic breath sets rows of cabbage out.

By that time it was easy to be sentimental about both the Indian and the Scout. Little boys, all over the white world, played in Indian dress and, reckless of historical accuracy, imported into the forest habitat of Seneca or Mohican the magnificent but, in that environment, quite impossible feather headdress of the Sioux or the Nez Percé. Buffalo Bill, from a scout, became a circus turn. While the last veterans of the old circus West were dying, the movies were born to make the American Sherwood Forest part of the world's great legends.

But the seriocomic ending of the great western movement should not blind us to its importance. It was one of the most decisive campaigns in world history; won in nearly three hundred years of ceaseless battle. And the unity of the great, central, fertile, and fantastically rich mass of North America had been fought for desperately, successfully. The almost invisible and practically impotent federal government of 1861 had survived one of the most desperate ordeals by battle that modern history has seen. Those political institutions that seemed incapable of minimum order, of minimum efficiency, that political system which seemed a mere amusement answered the question put by Lincoln, whether "a nation conceived in liberty and dedicated to the proposition that all men are created equal . . . can long endure." It did endure, and the losers in the great battle, with their bitter sense of defeat and their more bitter sense of exploitation and betrayal by the victors after their defeat, accepted the judgment of arms. It was Jefferson Davis who at the end of his long apologia for his cause and himself, put the motto *Esto perpetua*. However bitterly the ex-President of the Confederate States of America may have felt, none of his fellow-Southerners have ever again attempted to undo that "more perfect union" promised in 1789 by the Constitution to the struggling and straggling seaboard states when the greatest of European states was entering on that cycle of revolution from which neither France nor Europe has yet emerged. The United States have stayed united; the American people has been made.

2

IN THE COURSE of conquering America and so making Americans, habits were adopted out of urgent necessity which may have survived that necessity. There was, for example, the need for overstatement. To get settlers to move to America it was necessary to paint "America the golden" in very golden colors indeed. Very skilled hands undertook this necessary task: good prose writers like Richard Hakluyt; good or goodish poets like Michael Drayton; good story-tellers of the "when I was in Transylvania" school like Captain John Smith.

And once the voyage was made, the hazard of new fortunes undertaken, pride, exultation at one's own daring, recurrent optimism as new dreams replaced the old, led to the constant "sale" of America to the old world. For the genuinely adventurous type, for the man and woman whom nature had made ready for America, the exultation and the pride were genuine. Those who did not share in this pride and exultation were probably ill adapted anyway; they died or returned home or kept quiet. They had better, for from the beginning the settlers had no use for "knockers," for anybody who committed the crime of what was to be described in a later age as "selling America short."

The pioneer American had a real economic as well as emotional interest in growth, in encouraging the booster spirit. If he wanted to stay in the new settlement which he had chosen, he had an interest in other people's staying too. Only so could the profitable rise in values which he counted on be realized. Only so could money be borrowed on the future prosperity of the settlement. If the town refused to grow, if it, in fact, was written off as a failure and abandoned by any serious number of its residents, not only were the anticipated gains lost but real losses were suffered, especially after the Supreme Court put the federal government's power behind the claims of the buyers of municipal and county securities. It mattered little or nothing whether the loans had been prudently or even legally contracted; the Supreme Court, over the protests of that great Iowa jurist, Mr. Justice Miller, insisted on collection from the remaining inhabitants. And while the ingenious borrowers might be enjoying their capital gains in the interesting little town of Los Angeles, the less foresighted inhabitants of a town or county on the prairie were forced to pay or be sold up. They were in the position of a Russian village community under the Tsar from which a number of freed serfs had vanished, refusing to pay their share of the redemption price. Pessimism in such a world was treason. And as long as this boom spirit was flourishing, treason it remained. Thus, in a later age when the Florida land boom was collapsing, many communities made desperate, indeed magical efforts to persuade themselves and the world that values were holding up. And on July 4th, 1926, the city of St. Augustine, the oldest settlement in the United States, formally buried as an embodiment of that treasonable pessimism, "J. Fuller Gloom," with a funeral ceremony conducted according to the rites of the Chamber of Commerce.

But magic notwithstanding, land booms always burst. There have been few American cities in the last twenty years that have not had on their outskirts ambitious "developments" that have not come off at all, or have come off only after a long period of holding on. Sometimes, the holding on was no great strain. It may be assumed that the losses incurred during the period when only handsome street lamps and magnificent pavements marked most of the development of the old Rockefeller farm in Shaker Heights on the outskirts of Cleveland were no great strain on the Rockefeller fortune. But for less well-financed speculations, the period of holding on might be fatal. The first speculator has so often taken the rap. How few American railroads, how few New York hotels have not gone through the wringer! How profitable has been the job of receiver! Indeed, there have been times when the innocent investors have been forced to wonder whether "receiver"—meaning the recipient of stolen goods—was not merely a special case of "receiver" meaning the officer appointed by a complaisant court to take over and administer the bankrupt assets of great and small concerns alike. It would be unkind to say on what American railroad this incident occurred, but when I complimented a friend of mine on the improved service on his local railroad, he replied, with no conscious irony: "Oh, service has been swell since it went into receivership; the management can afford to spend money now that it hasn't got to worry about the stockholders." This was a commuter's view, not a stockholder's, but there has always been among Americans, including the luckless investors themselves, a philosophical acceptance of the fact that somebody must hold the bag for the great economic improvements of modern America.

The American farmer is perhaps rather less philosophical than the urban investor. He thinks he has a right to expect not a good living or a good cash income but a permanent and certain increase in the selling value of his land. It is this expectation that makes him hold on through drought and storm flood and tornado. On this expectation he borrows money and, as a permanent borrower, he has no fear of inflation; like the small boy in the story, far from being troubled by the thought he simply loves it. He knows, in a general, intellectual way, that somebody will have to be the last buyer, but he hopes and trusts that it won't be he. He will be living off the profits, perhaps invested in new lands, perhaps taken out in mortgages or in a rent that takes full account of the presumed value of the land, future as well as present. And the American absentee owner is not necessarily somebody like the late Lord Clanricarde, celebrated miser, tyrant, and last chief of the elder line of the Burkes, but a mild, modest ex-farmer living in decent comfort in the neighborhood of Los Angeles, raising the moral tone of the neighborhood and swelling the crowds at Iowa picnics. He may be simply a resident in a small Iowa town, able to afford a trip to St. Petersburg to pitch horseshoes in the winter sun of Florida. Or he may be like the Vermont farmer who, when asked by a scornful Midwestern visitor what crops were raised on those stony hills, replied: "The chief crop is those good five per cent Iowa mortgages we hold." The web of speculation, of optimism, of boosting is cast over all the nation.

But, of course, there was a real interest in persuading people to stay. The local banker made his money by backing rising values; he lost if they *all* fell. The local doctor who, like John Hay's father, chose the wrong town to settle in, paid for it in a life of comparative shallows and miseries. Hence the importance of prophetic statistics. "Albuquerque 40,000 by 1930." "Hamlet is a fine town, population 800."

I don't think Albuquerque made it by 1930, and I suspect that Hamlet had slightly inflated its figures. But editors of encyclopedias and guide-books have got to accept the necessity of printing not only the federal census figures, but the local estimate—which is always larger; millions of Americans appear to sleep out of town on census day.

One way of anchoring a settler is to get him married and settled down to raising a family. Hence the emphasis on good schools; lavish expenditure on school buildings is not necessarily a totally disinterested tribute to education; it is a bribe to wandering parents. But of course it would not be a bribe to parents who had not the inherited or acquired New England belief in education as a good thing. Even more effective anchorage was investment in a house—or, as the Americans say, a home. And expensive, highly ornamental homes were proof that the settlement was taking root. As Mark Twain put it long ago (in *Life on the Mississippi*): "Every town and village along that vast stretch of double river frontage had a best dwelling, finest dwelling, mansion—the home of its wealthiest and most conspicuous citizen." They still have, although today one would hardly expect to be believed if he asserted what Mark Twain asserted with no apparent fear of contradiction: "Not a bathroom in the house; and no visitor likely to come along who has ever seen one."

These optimistic exhibitions of civic pride have long been a British jest, a jest which sophisticated Americans have more recently joined in. But most Americans are still touchy on the subject of local improvements, as I discovered when I made an innocent joke about the Chicago drainage canal in a London paper. The European visitor lacks the eye of faith. Thus Dickens made Cairo, Illinois, the butt of his angry wit in his picture of "Eden" in *Martin Chuzzlewit*; but twenty years later, Anthony Trollope found that picture too flattering. "I doubt whether that author ever visited Cairo in midwinter, and I am sure he never visited Cairo when Cairo was the seat of an American army. Had he done so, his love of truth would have forbidden him to presume that even Mark Tapley could have enjoyed himself in such an Eden." * But only a quarter of a century after Trollope played the sourpuss, Cairo was given a big hand by a

* Anthony Trollope: *North America*, Vol. II, p. 121.

local resident. "Three years ago people said all the hateful things they could about Cairo. Now they are lavish in their praises. The paper says we'll monopolize all the trade of the Mississippi, Ohio, Tennessee and Cumberland Rivers. Our new grain elevator is one of the largest in the world, new railroads are constantly striking us. We've the most magnificent hotel (run on the grandest scale) in this part of the country, telephone system, new Opera House, elegant one, going up, street-cars soon to be running, and we are altogether citified."* So wrote a very bright, very nice local girl, a girl nicer and certainly much brighter than any Dickens or Trollope heroine I can remember. Cairo did not become a new St. Louis or Chicago, but "Maud" liked it and believed in it and what was good enough for her should have been good enough for any reasonable body.

This conception of growth as everybody's business, everybody's interest, is deep-rooted in the American national psychology. The bulky real estate supplements of the Sunday papers are no doubt largely kept going as an advertising revenue producer, but they would produce no advertising and no revenue if no one read them. The Englishman, hidden behind his hedge or wall, is not interested in his neighbor's house, and the idea of wanting to read about houses bought, sold, or built by total strangers is not even funny; it is merely absurd. But to an American, it is not only important, it is comforting, it is gratifying to know that other people are improving your home town; even people who have no personal economic stake in the rise of real estate values feel the same kind of interest that makes a motherly woman smile with genuine amiability on the children of total strangers. The very linguistic difference between "house" and "home" is significant. All Americans who live in houses, not apartments, live in homes; the Englishman lives in *his* home, but all his neighbors live in houses or flats.

The interest of the American in community growth is not confined to homes. He is far more aware of the size and importance of public and business buildings than anybody in England is. To the inhabitants of Minneapolis, the Foshay Tower was a symbol of growth, of maturity, that did not lose its value when the too enter-

* *Maud*, edited and arranged for publication by Richard Lee Strout (Macmillan), p. 22.

prizing *entrepreneur* went to jail. But in London, people do not long notice what new buildings have gone up and, after a month or two, find it hard to remember what stood on the site cleared by a German bomb. The idle, the curious are no more numerous in America than elsewhere, but those gazers on men-at-work on a new building whom the Americans call "sidewalk superintendents" are a more representative class of citizen than their English fellows. When John D. Rockefeller, Jr., built a covered-in observation post for the comfort of these spectators during the winter when Rockefeller Center was being built, he was not only acting with genuine American hospitality, he was recognizing a genuine and generous American interest in building as such. It is not at all unlikely that, among the spectators who watched with approving interest the new buildings which were rising with a speed that, by our standards, is really not very much slower than the speed with which Aladdin built his palace for the Princess, were stockholders in the Empire State Building. And they had nothing but a truly American tradition to encourage them to cheer the progress of a rival monument to the passion for the bigger and better—or, at any rate, bigger.

In pioneering conditions, personal credit—credit for courage, for competence, for industry, for economic promise—was all important. A pioneering community was composed of people all of whom were extending credit to each other as well as to the locality. When conditions were a little better, a little more settled, credit in the ordinary sense became important, but it was personal, too. The village banker in America was not in the position of the village usurer in Europe. His debtors could walk out on him; they were not anchored to the spot by tradition, by hereditary investment in land and family pride, by the difficulty of finding any place to go—except America. Indeed in Ireland, classic land of the village usurer, lending money to pay fares to America was one of the chief business opportunities—and risks. So there was a mutual assessment of need and greed. But the village banker, unlike the European village moneylender, was himself living on credit; and when it failed him, he might be the sudden migrant, leaving his debtors legally tied to his creditors, while he sought fresh woods and pastures new. Altogether, moneylending and borrowing was more of a sport in America than it was in Europe,

and banking, in the West at any rate, called for rather different qualities from what it demands from a citizen of London or a financier of
Wall Street. Mr. Ogden Nash's gloomy reflections on the parentage
of great American bankers are not, as far as I know, borne out by
the facts, but they fit the national tradition of classing bankers with
the other robber barons—though it must be remembered that these
robber barons were highly popular as long as they shared or were
believed to be sharing the spoil.

But one result of this necessity for and acceptance of the conditions of credit is that publicity must be accepted. If you want (as
most American women do want) to have a charge account or a series
of charge accounts, you must submit your husband's credit rating to
professional and competent investigation. It is of little use for the
American husband to try to obey the old maxim of folk-wisdom that
bids a husband keep secret from his wife the amount of money he
has, if she can, in effect, make a pretty good guess by trying to stretch
his credit at a department store. The general acceptance of debt,
however disguised, as a normal state of existence for many worthy
people no doubt leads to ostentatious expenditure, to conspicuous
waste, as it leads to non-functional automobile design and other specimens of art for show's sake. But it also leads to a fish-bowl existence
in which the English passion for privacy would offend public opinion
and constitute a luxury that only a very large independent income
could support. What I have been told of life in official circles in India
—that the public knowledge of the incomes of all the nice people cuts
out certain kinds of ostentatious expenditure—applies to many American communities, too. They all try to keep up with the Joneses, but
they are local Joneses, with accounts at local banks and stores. The
attempt to keep up with remote Joneses, to ape the manners and
expenditure of remote social circles, and the refusal to admit that
there is in that community anybody with whom it is really possible
to associate on terms of equality—this is more common in Streatham
than in Bronxville. American life imposes respect for the human
interest of the community in your private affairs; a refusal to con-
form at that level is, in fact, a vote of censure on the community
which it has no intention of submitting to. You can defy it, but at
the cost of being laughed at, not admired—and possibly at the cost

of having the local bank wonder if anybody so high hat can be a good risk.

It has to be admitted that this national spirit was often hard on dissenters—dissenters, that is, from the religion of economic and political optimism. A pioneer community could afford to house very hard citizens; it often benefited by the energies of persons who, to use modern terms, "cut their ethical corners rather fine." Courage, enterprise, ingenuity—these were qualities from which everybody benefited, or nearly everybody. So, in many ways, the frontier settlement was very tolerant. But it was not tolerant of the man whose arrogance or pride or morbid pessimism made him a nuisance in a society where all had to hang together if they were not to starve or be scalped separately. Pennsylvania could afford some Quakers, but not too many, in a great crisis like the French and Indian War; but the Revolutionary party in 1776 could not afford to be tolerant of too many Tories (i.e., Loyalists), since it was by no means certain how the majority would react to a strong lead. It was necessary, therefore, by legal or illegal violence, to give them a strong lead—and on one side only.

Religious dissent was more tolerable—as long as it was not dissent from the social creed of the growing nation, or disbelief in economic prosperity, or objection to military service, or real belief in the imminent end of the world. And dissenters or even "atheists" or "deists" were often very energetic and valuable citizens, promoters, and fighters. Indeed, it is possible that as things settled down, as communities acquired more coherence, the role of the religious or political dissenter got harder, since his other qualities became less necessary. But there remained legitimate grounds of dissent. After the Civil War any well-established village in New England or the northern Middle West could afford a town drunkard, a town atheist, and a few Democrats.

But a habit grew up in which it was necessary to call on some courage and perhaps on some independent economic resources before defying the local folkways. The very friendliness of American life made the dissenter more conspicuous. In a country where minding your own business is *de rigueur,* nobody need care what that business is. But in a country where all life is or should be lived pretty publicly, there is more intolerance of an individual eccentricity which is being continually thrust under the eyes of your neighbors. The high degree of social integration of a small American city (above a certain income level) plays its part, too. The tragedy of Mr. John O'Hara's *Appointment in Samarra* involves more than the weakness of the hero; it involves a life made intolerable if the country club and the local business community are mobilized against you. The highly individual character is a misfit in a community in any country, whether his weakness is genius or madness. If he has a private income like Cézanne, he may pursue his vision unmolested. But what Cézanne called "*les grappins*" are more tenaciously extended in America than elsewhere; they put out their tentacles more determinedly and a persistent evasion of their embraces is more offensive than it would be in a French or English town with no common social life anyway. There is truth in the picture of the Faustlike Professor in the film *On the Avenue*:

> *He attracted some attention*
> *When he found the fourth dimension.*
> *But he ain't got rhythm*
> *No one's with him.*
> *He's the lonesomest man in town.*

And since the common interest of the community is still assumed to be economic growth, attained by the "American way," the dissenter from the end, or the means, is especially open to suspicion. But 1929 wrought a great change, probably a permanent one. The sponsors of the old programs have not quite the same confident ring in their voices; too many things have been tried and have failed; the "American way" has been found to be a term less precise than it seemed in the presidential election of 1928 when the problem of poverty was solved and when the good citizens should have been busily expanding their garages to take the second car that was coming along with tomorrow's sunrise. Senator Robert Taft can, with a clear conscience, advocate the putting of the fiscal policy of the nation in the hands of practical men, since the last two Republican Secretaries of the Treasury are dead, but the memory of 1929-33 is a ghost that still walks. New Mellons and new Millses are ready in the wings, but the call has not yet come.

Nevertheless, the strident tone of American controversy, though not unparalleled in modern British history, is a reminder of a national tradition, pragmatically justified, in which dissent, especially continuous pessimistic crabbing, was near to treason. So the High School of Muncie teaches loyalty to Muncie as well as to the United States, and in less straightforward communities something of the same spirit prevails in more sophisticated forms.

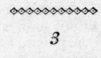

3

IT WAS NOT surprising that the Americans, at the end of their long march from ocean to ocean, should have too hastily assumed that they "had America licked." But it was an error, all the same. The continent remained not so much hostile as capricious; the gorgeous West, pouring out wealth with lavish hand, often had more than a hand inside the glove. The settlers in the South and in the Mississippi Valley had had to deal with diseases that, to northern Europeans, were very hard to manage. There was yellow fever, coming in from the West Indies; there was pellagra; there was hookworm; there was malaria. Some of these diseases became manageable as modern medical technology developed; Gorgas and Manson and Pasteur and Ross not only made the Panama Canal a possibility— they also made an easier and safer life possible in the continental United States. Pellagra is curable mainly through a rise in economic standards, and—so far as that has come about—pellagra has been cured; although in the poverty-stricken and decaying regions of the South it is still a menace to white and black poor alike—and a disease that makes life disagreeable in Umbria has even less to make it tolerable in the derelict regions of Georgia. Malaria needs fighting by cleanliness, and this, too, involves economic factors, for it is far harder for the poor to be clean than for the rich. Hookworm is highly debilitating, but you are much less likely to get it if you wear shoes—and shoes cost money; there is nothing romantic about being a barefoot boy in the hookworm belt. Improved water supply, improved medical services, even the rudiments of organized sanitation were necessary to turn the depressed and despised "mudsills" of the South—once denounced for their quite sensible habit of eating "dirt" (i.e., earth) as a remedy for the deficiencies caused by hookworm—into healthy and energetic citizens. The work of the Rockefeller Foundation and of the state and federal governments did more for this southern problem than cubic miles of southern oratory—although some excellent oratory was devoted to getting the South to accept northern aid. And among the many things which the New Deal set out to do for the South (where so many New Deal votes were cast and some New Dealers even got elected) was to subsidize the building of privies. When the federal government went into the same business as Lemuel Putt of Sangamon County, that was news—and good news.

But the South was especially handicapped, climatically, historically, racially, economically. The problem of making the Middle West habitable was much easier; it required wealth and energy and scientific knowledge, which the region acquired in abundance. It also required a high degree of political efficiency, which was not so abundant. The Chicago drainage canal, though a reasonably adequate solution for Chicago, was less attractive to her downstream neighbors. But other breakdowns only prove that human institutions are human; a local collapse of sanitary efficiency is no more to be wondered at in Chicago than in Croydon.

Even the most favored regions had their drawbacks. The first settlers who moved into the Pacific slope were richly rewarded. Oregon, reasonably warm, well wooded, well watered, was more like Devon than like Illinois. And California, to the pioneers coming over the High Sierra or round the Horn, was a new Canaan. Indeed, as the first Americans began to visit the Californian coast, the great empty land with its scattered Mexican ranches was more like the world of

Abraham than like the new machine world that already existed on the other side of the Atlantic. California cried out for more energetic settlers, and a swarm of Moses appeared to seize the land where, in its last spasm of imperial energy, Spain had created the little missions of San Francisco, Santa Barbara, San Luis Rey, San Luis Obispo, San Diego, and—destined to a highly paradoxical destiny—the village called after "Our Lady, Queen of the Angels." California had many attractions, but one struck home in the Great Valley: it had no malaria; "the shakes" were unknown. But, as the unkind Frenchman said of New Zealand, "There are no snakes, but a great many Scotchmen," and even California had its drawbacks. It had no weather, only the most perfect climate in the world, where season followed season in perfect regularity, with hardly an exceptional day. It seemed to be too good to be true. It was. The most regular feature of San Francisco weather was the summer fog, and in even more favored Southern California (as a saboteur from Florida put it in *The New Yorker*), "there is no rain, but the heavy dew sometimes washes away the railroad bridges." All around Los Angeles, the justification for this hit below the belt can be seen; empty river beds lined with concrete, provided with admirable bridges, recalling the Manzanares at Madrid. But the old joke to the effect that the Madrileños ought to sell the bridges and buy a river is pointless in the Californian outpost of New Spain, for when the rains do come, they come down with a speed and exuberance that are worthy of the Golden State; seven inches in two days makes very necessary indeed the bridges and parapets that control the *arroyos* turned torrents. Nor are floods the only trouble in California. The State has no equivalent of those terrible lightning storms of the Middle West, but it does have earthquakes. Significantly, it is still a little tactless to refer (in San Francisco) to "the earthquake of 1906"—you should say "the Fire," because that result of the natural catastrophe is less painful to recall. Fire is a manageable enemy of man and an old one, but when the foundations of the earth move, the most optimistic Californian is reminded of the untamable nature of the American land.

And at the other side of the continent, the rival paradise of Florida has had its bad shocks: in sudden frosts that kill the citrus crops; in devastating tornadoes that wreck the Miami waterfront as thoroughly as a second-class air raid could, or sweep the sea over such bold works of man as the road across the Atlantic to Key West.

In the other parts of America, the savage possibilities of the climate are never forgotten. All Ohio remembers the great flood year of 1913, whose impact on Columbus Mr. Thurber has made familiar to English readers. From that disaster came an elaborate and expensive system of flood control in Columbus, in Dayton, in all southwestern Ohio. But other river towns in other states have had their own and much more recent disasters. The Wabash does not, alas for the citizens of Indiana, always stay within its banks; and when we get to the Mississippi, we are faced with the greatest engineering problem in the western world. Only the great rivers of China have so bad a record. The floods starting when the ice and snow melt, fifteen hundred miles away from the subtropical delta, present a problem every year. And the news that is flashed down the river has the urgency of an air-raid alert, for ten feet of extra water at Paducah may mean disaster if something is not done *at once* at Vicksburg. So men and boys, white and black, are called out to pile cotton bales and sandbags on the threatened levees; women and children get ready to flee from the rising wall of water being funneled down the river. And somewhere the sides of the funnel give way and tens of thousands are made homeless, hundreds are drowned, and an economic catastrophe that would ruin a minor European state has to be coped with.

Even in the long-settled East, the water is still restive. The Connecticut River, normally as placid as the Thames at Teddington, sometimes goes on the rampage, reminding the inhabitants of cities like Hartford that life and property are still insecure. Great storms drive the sea over the summer cottages of Block Island. And there was an historical appropriateness in the comment Nature provided for the end of the tercentenary celebration at Harvard, for on the last day the great "storm wind of the equinox" that had been rushing up the coast from Florida struck Cambridge (Massachusetts) with a force unknown to Cambridge (England). It showed that for the sons of the Puritans the God of their Fathers was still an angry God of storm and rain like Him who had smitten the army of Sisera and had later toughened the New Englanders.

Even when there are no catastrophes, there are constant climatic problems. The mere range of temperature is a problem. How do you plan your life in a place like Bismarck, North Dakota, where the July temperatures have ranged between 32° F. and 108°, and the January temperatures between 45° below zero and 60° above? What do you do, even in normally kindly New Orleans, where the January temperatures have ranged between 15° and 82° and the July temperatures between 35° and 102°? In Wyoming at the source of the Colorado River, there is frost in every month of the year; over many states there is never any frost at all for decades at a time. *But* no part of the United States—not Texas, not Florida, not California—is free from frost that will, when by a freak it does come, kill lemons and oranges and avocados and break the hearts or strain the consciences of local boosters.

It seems likely that not until this century did the Americans really adjust themselves to the climate—as far as it is humanly possible to do so. Those who were of British origin were especially handicapped, coming as they did from an island where no one had been really comfortable in winter between the departure of the Romans and the coming of the more exigent type of American tourist. It is worth noting that one of the most important inventions of that most representative of Americans, Franklin, was an efficient stove (another was the lightning conductor). But to make houses even reasonably airtight was a problem; the log cabin, whether or not it was of Finnish origin, was a solution better than any that English practice would suggest. The continuous series of farm buildings—house, stables, barn, all in line so that the farmer could pass from the kitchen to the horses and on to the cattle without going into the bitter air—was another necessary adjustment; moreover, it provided a fine range of buildings that could be turned into rumpus rooms, garages, etc., when city folk took over the New Hampshire countryside. With primitive central heating, the last lap was entered on. It is possibly no accident, again, that the most modern thermostatic systems of central heating owe their essential equipment to a firm in Minneapolis where the winter cold can kill ten times as often as it can on the milder Atlantic. An Iowa farm, painted in midwinter by Grant Wood, with its red barn and dominating silo is highly functional: devoted to the job of keeping men and stock alive and food and feed usable through the long siege of winter. No American farm-bred boy or girl is likely to think that he or she has America licked.

Nor, indeed, is the town boy, who, as he grows up, will have at least one memory of a great and killing cold spell, even if it does not become so legendary as the great New York freezes of 1837 and 1888. Gardeners will long remember the late winter of 1933-34 which killed so many plants and shrubs on Long Island; and all regions of America, except the South and the Pacific Coast, have their own stories of death by cold, of stalled buggies or sleighs or even cars, of the dangers of bad chains or defective car-heaters, of a winter climate that always bears watching.

And summer demands it even more. For the early settlers were even less acclimated (as Americans put it) to heat than to cold. For one thing, as Professor S. E. Morison has pointed out, they wore far too many and too thick clothes. Even the Andalusians of Columbus' crews wore too many garments for a Caribbean summer. North Europeans did worse. There were economic obstacles, of course; until cotton textiles became cheap and abundant around 1800, linen was expensive and woolens uncomfortable. But there was more in it than that. Long after adequate textiles were abundant and cheap, fashion —not merely style but moral fashion—kept too many clothes on the American man and still more on the American woman. Men might wear "dusters" like Lincoln, or "seersuckers" like the prosperous middle class of the eighties. If they were prepared to be conspicuous, they might wear white linen suits like Mark Twain. But they still wore too much and, for dress occasions, they had to wear "Prince Alberts" (i.e., frock coats), tall hats, broadcloth, and starched collars and shirts. Theodore Roosevelt was regarded as pretty eccentric and reckless of the conventions, yet his typical costume was very formal and very uncomfortable indeed, compared with that of his niece's husband, the President of the United States today. It was still thought worthy of note when William Jennings Bryan took his coat off at Dayton, Tennessee, and defended Genesis in his shirt-sleeves—and that was not quite twenty years ago. And the uniform of the American army that went to France in 1917-18 included a stiff cloth collar that made the British officer's uniform the envy of his semi-strangled comrades in arms.

As for the women, to look at fashion magazines of 1900, to read in *Middletown* of the clothes worn in Indiana in the summer a generation ago, even to recall the fuss made about the length of bathing-suit skirts and other problems of sartorial morals twenty years ago, is to be as struck with astonishment as were the Greeks who learned from Herodotus that among the Lydians it was thought shameful even for men to be seen naked. No one, least of all a woman, need be overclothed in an American summer today. Indeed, unless she is clever with the needle or can afford custom-made clothes, any American woman who resolved to wear at least half as much as her mother used to would be baffled in any department store however big. The South Sea Islanders, put into "Mother Hubbards" by American missionaries and in consequence suffering discomfort, or even death, have been thoroughly avenged.

It is not only the American house that has at last been adapted to the American climate. American food has, too. Although Americans have always, by European standards, been abundantly fed, they have not until recently been well fed. One early difficulty of adjustment was that of diet; the average pioneer wanted the roast beef of old England or its equivalent, and was not to be put off with such new-fangled dishes as turkeys, tomatoes, corn, etc. He did adjust himself fairly quickly, but only in the sense of adding American items to European, not of balancing his diet or making it suit the climate and the work he had to do.

Of course some classes and some regions have been badly fed for economic reasons. "Hog and hominy," the diet of the Confederate army, was bad, but any other diet would have been a novelty to Southern poor whites. Negroes were and often are badly fed from any point of view. But travelers and critical Americans alike long lamented the monotony of American food, the good food ruined in that enemy to the pursuit of happiness, the frying-pan; the saleratus bread which was debited with the American sallow complexion and the melancholy view of life characteristic of many Americans in middle age. Until modern storage methods came in, the severity of both winter and summer made variety in diet difficult. Ice, indeed, was an early American passion; in water, in coffee, in juleps and other alcoholic concoctions. But it was ice cut and stored in a New England winter and shipped to South Carolina—and India—in a highly specu-lative voyage. For if most of your cargo arrived safe, your fortune was made, while if your ship was becalmed, all you had was extra water ballast of no market value. One of the minor hardships of the South-ern gentry in the War between the States was the shortage of ice, no laughing matter in the mint-julep country of tidewater Virginia.

With the coming of artificial ice, the worst was over and ice in summer became almost as necessary as coal in winter. European pio-neers made refrigerator cars possible, to the profit of the meat-packers of Chicago and the fruit-growers of California and Florida. But American men still ate too much meat, ate it too often, and did not balance it with sufficient fruit and vegetables. It is only in modern times, very modern times, that the American diet has become varied, light, and suitable for the climate. The electric refrigerator is becom-ing a necessity; deep freezing promises new culinary resources, and air conditioning promises a new climate—indoors, at any rate. There is no visible prospect of any method of obviating the Turkish-bath sensation that hits the person who goes out from an air-conditioned train or store or movie house on a very hot day. It is still too early to relax. America has always managed to keep her children on their toes; she still manages to do so. But the day is not in sight on which science and business together will be able to guarantee the climate and natural resources of California to the whole Union—or even to California.

4

BY THE END of the nineteenth century, the frontier era was over and the conquest and taming of the wilderness by American men and women entered into its modern phase of making rapid adjustments to a new way of life in which American men and women could take their ease in the Zion they had conquered and made to flow with milk and honey. It was certainly flowing more copiously than it had when the first scouts had reported. Though a long time was required to find it, there *was* gold in those mountains. And there was iron and coal and natural gas and copper and oil. Above all oil. The United States "struck oil" just under a century ago. From the earth came bursting out the unsuspected black gold, the simplest way known to man of conferring treasure upon a prospector. Wealth poured in on communities and individuals little better prepared than Osage Indians who were taken overnight from a thrifty life whose problem was to save, to a life where rational spending was the problem. It was no wonder that the extravagant spending of "Coal Oil Johnny" became traditional.

Nor was oil the only source of new wealth. There were the gold magnates who exploited California; there were the even more splendiferous silver magnates of the Great Bonanza. It was not only the father of Evalyn Walsh McLean who struck it rich—thousands did; in a sense the whole United States did. There was the Mesabi range in which you just scooped the iron out, like cheese. There was the mountain of copper in Butte, Montana, which made the fortunes of Sheridan, Kelly, and Clark and became the basis of the Anaconda. Fantastic mansions on Fifth Avenue and Nob Hill reflected the sudden wealth of prospectors like Flood and Clark and the more prudent businessmen who sold to and bought from prospectors. It was over the exploitation of oil that the first great modern economic controversy was raised; the Standard Oil was the first trust; the Rockefeller fortune, the first that really passed the dreams of European avarice. To monopolize the sources of such wealth was the key to power—and it meant denying to other would-be exploiters their chance of a share in the loot. Faced with these great corporations, the old common law, the old democratic machinery, seemed not even to belong to a horse-and-buggy age. They were almost pre-wheel.

But with native capital pouring out of the soil, with the paying-off of the European mortgage on American resources, with the parallel growth of industry and new techniques, the American man and, still more, the American woman entered on the more abundant life. Europe began to be outdistanced in wealth, in economic efficiency, in modernity. As late as 1867, when Mark Twain and the other tourists of the Quaker City went to Europe, they were visiting not only a continent full of interesting relics but a continent far more advanced in technique and wealth than the United States. A few years before, young Henry Adams had gazed with rather horrified interest at the English black country, as a train whirled him, far faster and far more comfortably than any American train could, from Liverpool to London. He knew that he was gazing at a sight unique in the world and in the history of the world. The American tourist, like Mark Twain, was overawed by the French railways and railway stations, by the wealth and display of the Paris shops. The Grands Magasins du Louvre were a sight as unparalleled in America as the Musée du Louvre. Effective systems of street lighting, of water supply, moderately clean streets and smooth roads—these were as much a European monopoly as Notre Dame or the Colosseum. Europe as a going concern was deeply impressive. The wealth of European magnates was stupendous. F. Bret Harte made his parody of Disraeli's *Lothair* turn upon the purchase of Chicago by the immensely rich young nobleman, Lothaw. There was even, a few years later, an agitation against wealthy Englishmen buying up large sections of the United States. How soon that changed!

The American woman was the chief gainer. No doubt most of the money originally passed through men's hands, but women had the spending of it. The American man was freed from most of the risks and back-breaking physical labors of crude pioneering, but the pioneer tradition of endless industry, of more and more, was unaltered by the change in circumstances. But to the heiress of the pioneer woman, the sewing machine, an effective system of heating, good oil lamps burning the good cheap oil sold by Mr. Rockefeller's octopus, running water in the cities, then in the towns, the coming of anesthetics and of less deadly childbearing, the appearance of an economic margin to spend on what had been luxuries and of time in which to spend the margin—these were really revolutionary changes. Of course they did not come all at once or universally over the country. In some backward regions they have not come yet. The last great frontier movement, which led to the settlement of the High Plains, inflicted as much hardship on the pioneer Scandinavian settlers, espe-

cially on the women, as any previous movement had done. To survive a winter on the plains, in a "sod house" dug out of the soil, called
for the qualities of giants in the earth as truly as surviving in a half-
faced camp in Kentucky had done. But the revolution spread rapidly.
President Folwell of the University of Minnesota died full of energy
a month before the bull market broke in 1929. Yet he could well
remember that his mother, in up-state New York, had set herself off
from many of her neighbors by never using "sluts"—that is, rag floating in fat and burning in a dish. She always used candles which she
made herself, till the sperm-oil lamps came into use. The development of the mail-order house with its ready-made clothes lightened
women's labor, as the sewing-machine had lightened it earlier. There
is less of a jump from ordinary baker's bread to modern bread,
wrapped in cellophane and sliced, than there was from the heavy
chore of home baking to baker's bread.

The American kitchen was well on the way—the first primitive
washing-machines; the first efficient ice-boxes; the telephone for
public gossip on the party line; the new plumbing; sinks designed to
break fewer backs; lighting planned to ruin fewer eyes; gas stoves,
then electric ranges, to reduce the strain of cooking. The can-opener
became a standard article of equipment and the basis of jokes for
hardworked comedians. In time, indeed, an efficient can-opener reduced the last hazards of kitchen work. The day of the Hoover
cleaner agent and the Fuller brush man was at hand. So, too, was
the day of leisure. The pioneer American feminists had to be Mrs.
Jellybys or spinsters. It was impossible both to set the world to rights
and to keep house with the old equipment. But by 1900, the American woman had been liberated (apart from the great majority who
were farmers' wives or wives of manual workers) from the worst
servitudes of her sex. Without any very public campaign urging it,
birth-control (or what President Theodore Roosevelt had called "race
suicide") was adopted; there were fewer children, and there was far
more time to devote care to them. The diet of Junior became a serious
preoccupation, and the need to straighten Sister's teeth. So did the
public schools, at which both of them might pick up foreign accents
or worse. So did the summer camps to which they could thankfully
be sent. The change was not sudden until the moderate-priced car

came; it merely marked the emergence of the American mother, a Martha solicitous now over only two things: her children (or child) and the world. It was as much as ever the duty of the husband to be a "good provider" and, as real incomes rose, what had been luxuries became necessities—especially if the children needed them.

As long as the American land was not completely settled, the elements of civilized order not yet imposed on the frontier, the permanent American passion for dealing in futures was devoted to prophetic brooding on material expansion and to prodigious efforts to make those prophecies either come true or turn out to have underestimated what could be done. But with the closing of the frontier, the discounting of the future took a more human form: it became the ambition of the American man and woman to provide a world in which life should be easier for the next generation. And as the closing of the frontier meant—psychologically if not materially—a closing-in of the horizons, since it was no longer possible to dismiss the problem of youth's economic future with a brisk "Go west, young man, and grow up with the country," the provision of a world in which young men and women could grow up in a fairly stable country became a national preoccupation. It was reflected in the increasing interest in, belief in, and credulity about education. It was reflected in the sharp fall in the size of the family. If, on the other hand, the old farm and village tradition survived that every boy, no matter how well off his parents, did chores at home and earned a little money outside, it gradually came to be slightly artificial. When the merchant's or the lawyer's son made some extra money by delivering papers or mowing lawns or (most serious chore of all) tending furnace, this was—like fagging in English public schools—a disciplinary ritual rather than a strictly economic function. The boy who was made to earn a dollar or two a week in such ways might be arguing, with tenacity and success, for the right to a car of his own or to a free hand with the family car.

As sons and daughters grew fewer, they were indulged more liberally—a phenomenon not confined to America. The American mother with only one or two sons was more hopeful of making a world fit for them to live in than the mother of six or seven could easily be. The very age limits of childhood shifted upwards. In New

England a century ago, men barely out of their 'teens were commanding clippers on voyages to China. The youthful character of American life struck visitors. Dickens was not exaggerating much when he took for children the young married couple in Martin Chuzzlewit's boarding house. A young man like MacKenzie could leave West Point during the Civil War and end it as a corps commander. But in modern America there is far more reluctance to admit that real maturity has come than there was even forty years ago. The excessive length of American professional education, which prevents a young doctor or lawyer from earning his living, or even beginning to earn it, until he is twenty-eight or older, may have something to answer for. So may the prolongation of youthful habits and ambitions into middle age which justifies the title of "girls" assumed by the plump matrons of Miss Helen Hokinson's art. But there has been a real shift in meaning between the days when "the boys in the back room" meant *anybody,* and our modern times in which robust and vigorous young men are called "boys" and treated as boys. Youth has become scarcer and more precious, and the natural and touching desire to shield the young, more uncritical and overpowering. So the Republican platform of 1940 was not ill designed—and probably not devoid of real meaning and feeling—when it recalled that "we are still suffering from the ill effects of the last World War; a war which cost us a twenty-four-billion-dollar increase in our national debt, millions of uncollectable foreign debts, and the complete upset of our economic system, in addition to the loss of human life and *irreparable damage to the health of thousands of our boys.*"

5

THE ADOPTION of the woman's thrifty view of human life, as compared with the extravagant masculine attitude, was only one sign among many that American society was moving from its frontier condition in which, no matter what theories were advocated, life had to be governed by masculine standards. Only a century ago, it is odd to remember, not merely were American women excluded from open politics as they were in England, but the Puritan standards generally accepted in American life denied them that illicit—or, at any rate, unofficial—influence which some English women exercised. I cannot think of any woman who played an important role in American politics before Peggy O'Neale induced President Jackson to champion her premarital chastity and thus forced a quarrel between the President and those members of his cabinet who had wives and so had to support the severest standards of female decorum—all to the profit of that subtle widower, Martin Van Buren, who thus became heir apparent to the presidency. But even society had comparatively little place for women, despite the social graces of the sprightly Dolly Madison. Men preferred to talk to each other and leave the women to themselves—a barbarous custom that shocked Mrs. Trollope, Miss Martineau, and other female visitors from the then more advanced country of England. Mrs. John Adams might complain that all men would tyrannize over their wives if they dared; it was not until the reforming forties that women's rights—with abolitionism, spiritualism, socialism, Mormonism, and transcendentalism—testified to the breaking-up of the orthodox ice that, for two centuries, had restrained the ardent spirits of New England. And only twenty years or so later, Lincoln could say to the author of *Uncle Tom's Cabin:* "So you are the little woman that caused this great war."

When the tide began to flow, it flowed rapidly. With *Little Women* and *The Battle Hymn of the Republic,* Frances Willard and Lucy Stone, the American woman was no longer silent. Even the business woman began to appear, in the ambiguous form of the Claflin sisters and then in the form of the classical American miser, Hetty Green. And if the religious movements of the pre-Civil War period, like Mormonism and Perfectionism, had found a place for women, it was in the post-war period that the most original development of American religious optimism was announced by Mary Baker Eddy.

The law which had pressed hard on women for so many generations now began to press hard on men. Marriage continued to be a lottery, but the law no longer allotted all the blanks to women. Divorce became easier and alimony more abundant. The first effective women's colleges, Vassar and Mount Holyoke, were founded or developed out of schools. State universities began to admit women on equal terms, and some western states gave them the vote. The woman doctor and the girl "prophet" of *The Bostonians* were both typical products of this age.

And the American woman began to clean up America, to make it less dirty, less sinful, less a boarding house for bachelors and more a home. The towns were taken in hand first; the farmer's wife had, as yet, not enough leisure to reform the countryside.

An example of the conquest of the American town by the American woman was the successful campaign against the toleration of organized prostitution, the tacit or open earmarking of an area of a city as a "red light district." Novels and films have now given us a kindlier view of this solution of the sexual problem than was generally held when it was in its glory. The *entrepreneuses* of the brothels, the "madams" of the "sporting houses" were all, we now learn, ladies under the skin, their hearts as golden as their hair. This was doubtfully true in some cases; and, even if it was true in a majority of cases, the whole attitude involved in this solution was an affirmation of that exclusion of American women from the whole of life against which they fought. The brothel, like the saloon, was a challenge to the American woman's passion for reducing masculine disorder and moral anarchy to reasonable limits (reasonable by female standards). Men were trying to have it both ways: to demand from "good" women rigorous standards of ignorant decorum,

and in addition to have license for themselves. The American woman
who had played—and who knew she had played—so great a part in
creating American society, and who proposed to play an even greater
part in moulding it, was not disposed to lie down under this threat,
this insult. And, in practice, long before women got the vote, it was
politically already very risky to cater too openly to the brothel interests, whatever lesser breaches of political decency like selling traction
franchises might be pardoned to the political machine if it were
otherwise respectable—i.e., Republican in the North, Democratic in
the South.

Campaigns against organized vice were waged over and over again,
mixed up with mere campaigns against indecent books and pictures.
But the opinion is hazarded here that American women did not
really worry much about banning books or pictures; "September
Morn" left them cold. The test case was the brothel and its political
tie-up, and even more the cynical and (from a feminist point of
view) contemptuous arguments with which the existence of such
an institution was defended or palliated. When the great department store, Macy's, moved uptown and built its vast new store on
the site of some of the most famous brothels in New York, the early
twentieth century opened with an omen of a new triumph for the
American woman. And few are the cities in which the old system
survives today, even in a disguised form. Few are the cities in which
open street-walking is as much a national institution as it is in Britain.
The "love-nest" is known; the visit to the local tourist camp for the
night is known; little "dens of iniquity" such as that which housed
the hero of *Pal Joey* are known. But not merely are these at least formally secret, not merely does vice pay the real homage of more or
less expensive hypocrisy to female and sometimes to male virtue, but
in all these illicit arrangements there is no element of undisguised
official toleration and there is no double standard of morality. In
America, as in England, that old dispute is over, for the time being
anyway. The war between the sexes is now fought on the level, even
if it is a low level by nineteenth-century standards.

But the great triumph of the American woman was prohibition.
It is true that many American women had by 1919 become sophisticated enough to like a drink themselves. But there was more wit

than statistical truth in the jest (possibly Mrs. Parker's) that "the American woman got the vote just too late to save the old-fashioned saloon." It is true that nowadays very few saloons, however old-fashioned, dare exclude the ladies, and those that do are likely to be treated with the scorn which, so I have been told, American ladies at Pompeii and Naples met Italian attempts to exclude them from the more curious relics of the culture of imperial Rome. But whatever may be the case today, a generation ago, two generations ago, the American woman declared and waged war on drink. It was the great enemy of her social and economic security. The bottle rather than the blonde was the rival she had to fear for her husband's income and for his otherwise certain devotion to his children. Strong drink was abundant and cheap; mere beer and wine are nineteenth-century importations into the American diet. Whisky, as has been said, was the chief export of the primitive frontier, and whisky was only one of numerous tipples. There were peach brandy and apple jack, white mule, Jersey lightning, Medford rum and Bourbon and rye whisky. For long, they were lightly taxed and fantastically cheap. Social life depended on them; great men like Daniel Webster lived on them, more or less. Even the clergy were not debarred from enjoying them. European drinking habits in the curious combinations of climates known in North America often produced catastrophic results. Hot buttered rum to keep out the winter cold, mint juleps to keep out the summer heat—these were drastic solutions for a serious climatic problem.

Drink was an occasion of sin and a cause of waste. Not only was it customary for newspapermen to go off for a week or two of hard drinking, but even such dignified persons as department store buyers who went out to lunch with customers often failed to come back. Mr. Saroyan's hero who held up the alcoholic arms of the telegraphist had his analogue in every American town and village and in practically all professions. Whether President Johnson and President Grant were drunkards, or merely had very poor heads for liquor, was the subject of much bitter political controversy. And it is perhaps significant that the first time the White House had to undergo the rigors of a dry regime was when Grant's successor, Rutherford B. Hayes, announced that since neither he nor Mrs. Hayes had approved of serving liquor in Columbus (Ohio), they would not change their habits in Washington, D. C. After that, as Secretary of State Evarts put it, water flowed like champagne in the White House. No subsequent President made such an issue of the liquor question as had President Hayes; but, whatever sophisticated half-foreign dwellers in Washington may have thought, millions of Americans warmly approved of the Hayes gesture—and their number increased.

The first prohibition wave which marked the period of ecstatic reforming before the Civil War ebbed. Only Maine, first to go dry, kept the law on its statute books, and it was perhaps in homage to the ethos of his adopted state that James G. Blaine had a report that he was "suffering from gout" amended to read "suffering from rheumatism." Even in the capital of moral reform, Boston, the dry laws were openly defied. It was, so the story runs, in one of the best Boston hotels that a classical rebuke was administered to a melodramatic pessimist who asked what he could do if a friend, say from St. Louis, wanted a drink. "I should say: *'Fils de Saint Louis, montez au ciel,'*" replied the realist, pointing to the floor above where there was a well-equipped speak-easy.

This defiance of the law, whether the defiance took the form of tolerating prostitution or tolerating liquor, was resented by the women, who found masculine indiscipline intolerable. It is true that such defiance was often not merely anarchical. There were substantial profits to be reaped by somebody, even by a community as a whole. Some students hold that the economic predominance of Seattle over its rivals on Puget Sound is due to the initial start it got from the popularity of its tolerated and famous brothels among the sailors and lumbermen of the last frontier. One otherwise undistinguished economic center, Moorhead, Minnesota, for long owed a good deal of revenue to its role as a licensed Alsatia in an area of legal Puritanism. St. Paul was frowned on by its neighbor Minneapolis for its worldly tolerance. The New England moralists of Greeley, Colorado, had no liking for the wide-open character of Denver. And the sins of San Francisco were long a cause of mournful pride to most of California and of a combination of contempt and envy to Los Angeles. But prohibition of liquor, of prostitution, even of cigarettes, was warmly advocated by the most vocal American women. All tobacco users (i.e., snuffers as well as smokers) were regarded as doubtful characters; and, as for smoking by women, that was a proof either of complete social squalor—as among the female pipe smokers of the southern Appalachians and Ozarks—or of definitely sinful propensities. It is only within the last fifteen years or so that cigarette manufacturers have been able to get away from subterfuges, such as making a pretty girl say "Blow the smoke my way," and to come out and face the fact that most young American women smoke.

The slackness of male enforcement of these taboos led to direct action. Carry Nation broke up the saloons of Kansas, then those of other states, finally carrying her crusade as far as Glasgow. And by the Eighteenth Amendment and the Volstead Act, the sale of beverage alcohol was made illegal all over the United States, even in sinful cities like New York and Chicago. There is no need to go into the sad history of what Mr. Hoover called "an experiment noble in purpose." The limits of mere law were revealed. The old frontier habit of shooting it out turned to the East, and the old circus act of holding up the Deadwood Coach was repeated, not in fun, on hundreds of new concrete highways. The authority of state and federal governments was made ludicrous, and regions and sections of society which in modern times had never really known the open use of alcohol, saw the naïve hypocrisy of highly alcoholic remedies for aches and pains replaced by openly sinful bathtub gin and moonshine. As prohibition was mainly a women's triumph, imposed on the reluctant politicians by fear of the women's vote, the failure of the experiment should have been highly educational. It showed that there were limits to the degree to which the old Adam could be expelled by noble purposes; it revealed some of the realities below the façade of mere voting. The laws, voted by women and evangelical zealots, were enforced by policemen and other legal instruments, and few of these had any belief in the desirability of drying America by law—or in any other way. It was the belief of many intelligent supporters of prohibition that a generation of boys and girls would grow up who, not knowing the taste of alcohol, would not want to drink—and perhaps the belief was not entirely foolish. Because no one could hold such a view about sex appetites, moral legislators in that field had always known that they had their work cut out for them. But the prohibition experiment never got a fair chance, since no generation of American adolescents had ever had more real alcoholic temptation put in its way than the generation that grew up during the years when booze was news—daily, dramatic news.

There is a close parallel between the optimism that led to the enactment of prohibition and the optimism which welcomed that international Volstead Act, the Kellogg Pact. In that optimism there was a strong element of the old-time religion, of belief in the old evangelical mass conversion. Hundreds and thousands had renounced the world, the flesh, and the devil in Kentucky or in the "burned-over" district of New York State; why should not the nations renounce mutual murder? And this conversion involved no serious mental stock-taking, involved no more than a firm resolution that the United States would not attack any nation and a belief that no nation would attack any other—especially the United States. That peace requires positive as well as negative action, that works as well as faith are needed, were ideas unwelcome in those golden days when, drink and poverty having been put on the road to extinction, war was scheduled as next to go. General amiability, a Good Neighbor policy that it was hoped would spread—these were to be enough. It was not that the other signatories to the pact were trusted implicitly, but it was obviously such good morals and such good business to renounce war! That there were rulers of peoples, in power or soon to be in power, who took a different view of morals was ignored. So, too, was the fact that it was all very well for President Coolidge to announce that "the business of the United States is business." Other powerful peoples did not agree that their business was exclusively business. What was at most true of American society at one moment in its history was taken as universally true. It was soon not even true of the United States. But for a time these illusions concealed from the American people, especially from the American woman, a truth enunciated by Mr. Dooley at the beginning of this belligerent century. As he pointed out, you can refuse to love a man, you can refuse to play with him, you can refuse to lend him money —but, if he wants a fight, you have got to oblige him.

War, even more than drink, was an absurd relic of man's barbaric and disorderly past. It was destructive; it destroyed what women made: children and homes. It led to waste of national resources on armaments. It was a purely masculine activity, and in every society in which it was a main activity it was inevitable that the position of women (the infallible index of civilization, so nearly every American woman believed and nearly every American man professed to believe) should be inferior.

And those who, like William James, looked for a moral equivalent for war were put off with violent games such as unreformed college football in which the players' armor underlined its adequately "dangerous" character as the American parallel of the bull fight. In campaigns for all kinds of objects military metaphors were freely used, and the American tradition of processions, of demonstrations, of massed emotional meetings, going back to the frontier camp-meeting and the frontier political campaign, provided substitutes for real military parades; so did military uniforms and military nomenclature.

The combination of a profound hatred of war and militarism with an innocent delight in playing soldiers is one of these apparent contradictions of American life that one has to accept. The American state universities for the most part started as land-grant colleges—that is, they were given large areas of federal land to subsidize education in agriculture and the mechanic arts. But, as the grants were made during the Civil War, military training was demanded, too. The American Army, once the South was conquered, shrank to a few thousands again; the militia was merely an amateur police force; nevertheless, military training of a kind remained a vague obligation of the state universities. It was not necessarily very functional. I myself have been served in a university restaurant, a few months after Pearl Harbor, by students wearing movie-usher uniforms plus swords; they were going on a parade as soon as the washing-up was done. The possibilities of exhibiting female legs in vigorous action provided by making "majorettes" (high-stepping and high-spirited young women) the chief feature of a college military band have not been neglected, and one of the most eminent American social critics has given us a highly plausible account of military training at Ohio State University during the earlier German war. "We drilled with old

Springfield rifles and studied the tactics of the Civil War even though the World War was going on at the time. At 11 o'clock each morning thousands of freshmen used to deploy over the campus, moodily creeping up on the old chemistry building. It was good training for the kind of warfare that was waged at Shiloh, but it had no connection with what was going on in Europe. Some people used to think there was German money behind it, but they didn't dare say so or they would have been thrown in jail as German spies." *

An apparently odder example of innocent militarism is provided by the military schools. These are not schools preparing for the army, or with a strong army tradition like Haileybury or Wellington, and are not to be confused with real military academies for training officers like the Virginia Military Institute or the Citadel at Charleston, South Carolina. They are simply boarding schools organized on military lines. They may be described as English public schools organized round the O.T.C. instead of the cricket team. The boys wear uniforms, uniforms a good deal more dashing than those of the American Army or even of the Marine Corps. School spirit is translated into military terms; the "Buckle down, Woonsockie, buckle down" type of song is set for bugles. Military methods of command are relied on to discipline the boy who is a handful at home, and a certain amount of elementary military training is provided. To see the Eton O.T.C. learning the manual of arms in what Americans call "cutaways" is to realize how much better they do such things at Culver. But there is no real military indoctrination, no militarism, no resemblance to the "leader schools" of the Third Reich, nor even to the slightly fevered atmosphere of the old United Services College as seen by the retrospective Kipling in *Stalky & Co.* I don't know of a Quaker military school, but I really don't see why there shouldn't be one.

There was some pacifist agitation against compulsory military training in colleges. Probably some parents decided against sending their boys to military school because it *was* military. But both college and school military training were so obviously unmilitarist in spirit that only the most morally sensitive really felt strongly about it. To worry about the militarization of young America was about as foolish as to worry about those colonels' commissions that Governor Ruby Laffoon

* James Thurber: *My Life and Hard Times* (Harper), p. 123.

of Kentucky was showering on every girl and on most men who got within hailing distance of the capitol at Frankfort. Never did America more determinedly *not* raise its boys to be soldiers than in the years before the coming of the most terrible foreign war in American history.

The American people, it must be repeated, have always been anti-militarist but never anti-military. They have combined a rational and civilized horror of war's waste and inhumanity with a simple and, for peoples of European origin, natural pleasure in the trappings of war. Their view of what constitutes the due "pride, pomp, and circumstance" of warlike parade is not that of the English or the Germans or the Japanese, but it is genuine all the same.

Nevertheless, the survival of this pleasure in the circus side of warlike activity and a great deal of rather naïve patriotic enthusiasm about the past was accompanied, between 1919 and 1939, by an equally vociferous zeal for perpetual peace and a refusal (equaled only in Britain and the British dominions) to see that peace could not be bought by mere resolutions of good behavior—might indeed call for such efforts of self-discipline and self-criticism that war would come to seem almost preferable.

As has been suggested, the growing and deserved power of American women had something to do with this attitude. So had a genuine and very justifiable optimism about America and a natural and in many ways admirable pride in the facts that so much of the world had now come to school to America, and that the prestige of American ways of life was so high. Had not a distinguished Frenchman, M. André Siegfried, said that the world would have to choose between Henry Ford and Gandhi? And few were the Americans who believed that, if the choice were given, any serious number even of the most benighted foreigners would choose Gandhi. And even if they did, the one thing Ford and Gandhi had in common was pacifism.

In the growth of this attitude there was, however, one factor of overwhelming importance: the widespread, almost universal American belief that intervention in the war of 1914-18 had been a luxury, and a foolish luxury at that. No nation likes being "played for a sucker"; no nation likes to think that it has been the victim of a gang of international spiritual comrades of Mr. W. C. Fields, all resolved not to give the American sucker an even break. American slang is rich in terms to describe the fate of the victim of the con man. America, so the American people was soon told, had been robbed by international crooks who had found the job of swindling her appointed guardians no more difficult than "rolling a lush." America was the lush, and the booze that had made her so easy a victim of international pickpockets was propaganda.

For the student of that art, the history of the American campaign of propaganda against propaganda must always rank as a masterpiece. Compared with the agents of Britain whom they denounced, the propagandists against propaganda were real masters commenting on the daubs of well-meaning amateurs. Like their British predecessors of 1914-17, the American artists were often perfectly sincere, not merely bringing more learning, more talent, and more knowledge of the market to the job, but doing all this with a conviction of moral superiority that the most naïve Briton could not have excelled. It is possible that some of the leaders in this campaign were slightly cynical. After all, it was in more than one way not unprofitable to see the world through German spectacles. Others were animated by the natural human reaction, especially natural in the young, against believing all or much of what your pastors and masters have told you. And lastly it was to the interest of the Republican party to discredit the policy of the Democratic administration. "The war is a failure" was the Democratic party line invented to discredit Lincoln in 1864. "The war was a fraud" was the slogan of Republican Vallandighams in 1920 and later.

But there was in American resentment a genuine moral element. The world had not been safe for democracy (Chesterton's reminder at the time that it could not be, that making it so was a dangerous trade, had been ignored). In many ways the world got worse while the United States got better, and even when the smash of 1929 proved that the American way of life could go backwards, too, it was natural to blame some exterior force. All the nations that had suffered from the war of 1914-18—victors and vanquished alike—naturally found comfort in blaming outsiders, with a good deal of justice since the outsiders *were* blamable. So a situation was created in America in which candid thought about the late war was made almost as difficult as it was in any of the countries that had suffered far more deeply.

It is the comparatively slight statistical impact of the last war on America, set in dramatic contrast to the psychological impact, that makes it hard for the foreigner to be just to the American revulsion from that war and from all wars that seemed like that war. American losses in life were far less, both absolutely and in proportion to the population, than American losses in the Civil War. The American motor car was a far more efficient killer of American youth than the German army had been. Some not very large towns in England and Scotland had suffered more fatal casualties than some American states. Yet the feeling that there had been great waste and *mere* waste was genuine. These American boys need not have been killed at all. A boy killed by a speeding car died a natural death; a boy killed in the Argonne was killed by propaganda, but for which he would have stayed at home.

Again it must constantly be remembered that before this war no nation had ever fought on such a scale so far from home—and now it is again the Americans who are fighting on the greatest scale far from home. True, this is in itself an advantage to America. The people of London learned in 1940 what the French learned in 1914-18, that it is no matter for rejoicing to have a war on your own doorstep. If the real interests of the United States were involved in either of these wars, the American people were to be congratulated on keeping the river of destruction away from their door. But simple people in any country refuse to reason that way. The remoteness of the battlefields, the thought that their sons were going into exile as well as into battle, was painful to American fathers and mothers. The thought of their dying so far from home was more bitter than the thought of their simply dying. The French soldier of Napoleon's army, dying on the retreat from Moscow, whose only complaint was, "It's a long way to Carcassonne," expressed a universal and ancient attitude: *"dulcis moriens reminiscitur Argos."*

Even had the world of 1919 onwards been obviously a great improvement on the world of 1914, the American people might have succumbed to the temptation to do some excessively rigorous political bookkeeping. But as it was, the theory that all this waste and suffering *could* have been avoided was sure to be readily welcomed, and it was. And the simplest form of the mere waste theory was the belief that propaganda had dragged America into a mess she had not made and in whose cleaning up she had no serious interest.

An eminent Victorian rationalist, it is asserted, once refused to "plaster the fair face of truth with that pestilent cosmetic, rhetoric." Something of the same vehement passion for truth in political advertising overcame the enemies of propaganda. In their zeal for calm, objective, disinterested statement of the truth, they were themselves at times betrayed into what was rather like the style of the much abused propagandists. "In the Great Society it is no longer possible to fuse the waywardness of individuals in the furnace of the war dance; a new and subtler instrument must weld thousands and even millions of human beings into one amalgamated mass of hate and will and hope. A new flame must burn out the canker of dissent and temper the steel of bellicose enthusiasm. The name of this new hammer and anvil of social solidarity is propaganda. Talk must take the place of drill; print must supplant the dance. War dances live in literature and at the fringes of the modern earth; war propaganda breathes and fumes in the capitals and provinces of the world." * At first sight this reads like a description of a jitterbug session, but for all its Corinthian exuberance of style it is an admirable piece of propaganda against propaganda. For it suggests to the impressionable reader that propaganda can work only one way—in the direction of action, *undesirable* action. Whether desirable action can be stimulated, or whether desirable action is above the need of stimulation, or whether inaction (the adoption of a generally sceptically indifferent attitude) is a good thing or a preservative against obviously bad things—these were questions that the average forward-looking writer did not put, questions which, if they were put, he did not stay to answer or hear answered.

The American people had, of course, many other reasons for scepticism. There was a considerable waste of simple faith and trust in the advertising world, not so much because the standard of advertising

* Professor Harold D. Lasswell: *Propaganda Technique in the World War*, quoted in James R. Mock and Cedric Larson: *Words That Won the War* (Princeton University Press).

veracity went down (actually it went up), but because the seriousness with which advertising was treated led to a general customer's attitude: "You've got to show me"—and the customer, bidden to think hard or dangerous or unpleasant thoughts, naturally asked to be excused. All the heart-warming epithets left over and still usable were quickly debased by their excessive employment in football pep talks. The naïve student whose "I'd die for dear old Rutgers" got an easy laugh was replaced by the cynical student whose unwillingness to believe in or act for any cause was taken as a proof of sophistication. The old were afraid to profess and the young too shy to admit any generous sentiments at all. Ill-understood words like "semantics" were bandied about; never was a generation so much under the influence of rhetoric, of mere words, as that American student generation that prided itself on standing, clear-eyed and cold, on a mountain top from which it could look down on the gullible generations of the near and distant past. Young people make very poor cynics, very poor realists; and the American young were no exception. But since the young hate being out of the fashion of their own age, a determined hardboiledness became the only tolerable wear, a sort of ideological equivalent of crew-cut hair and brogues.

The arguments advanced by the enemies of the policy of the Wilson administration—and accepted by many of its friends—were not merely convenient, they were plausible. American intervention in 1917 had been represented in two lights, neither of them of sufficient candle power to make the whole picture clear. There was the view that promises of good behavior made by the Germans had been broken, that the dignity of the United States had been attacked, that the flag had been fired on, that American men, women, and children had been murdered on the high seas on their lawful occasions. That view was true as far as it went. It was a powerful stimulant to emotional action while the old, simple view of national dignity and honor was still powerful. But just as the firing on Fort Sumter and on the flag was only the occasion of the Civil War not its cause, so the German submarine campaign was not a real cause. The German government's use of the submarine was not merely meant as a reprisal for the British blockade—it aimed at the destruction of British military power by naval means, by the naval means open to the lesser naval power. The calculation that this was the best and cheapest way to win the war even if it brought the Americans in was deliberately made. Only the Americans' acceptance of whatever this policy involved—and, far more important, their acceptance of whatever consequences the success of this policy involved—would have saved the United States from war.

This was evident to acute American publicists, to students of public policy. Some were willing to take the risk of a German victory, some were not. Some believed that there was no real risk of such a victory anyway; others, that the United States could get along in a world in which sea-power and land-power were united; still others, that unpleasant though such a world would be and expensive though living in it would prove, the cost of averting such disasters by entering the war on the side of Britain and France was excessive. It does not always pay to insure; the premium may be too high.

But the American people, used to the idea of immunity, their eyes turned inward by centuries of historical necessity, ill informed as to the issues of power involved, and sceptical as to the risks for the United States of any shift in the balance of power, could not be moved to action by any such reasoning. "One Yankee could lick any ten foreigners"—and this argument was even advanced about navies—a quarter in which gallantry is no substitute for ships. By 1914, the only naval power in a position to threaten the dominance of the British Navy was the German, not the American; despite this fact, it was believed that—as a writer in *Munsey's Magazine* put it, the superior qualities of the officers and men would more than compensate for the inferior number of battleships and the complete absence of battle cruisers.

The American people has to be stirred to action by an emotional cry, and doubtless it was greatly stirred by the insult to the flag when its ships were fired on by German submarines. But it was not stirred quite enough to generate the emotional temper required for stronger action than the mere arming of merchantmen or the convoying of shipping. The "little group of willful men" in the Senate who filibustered against the armed-ship bill were probably as unpopular with the majority of the American people as they were with President Wilson, but they would have been more numerous and less willful if they had been opposing the sending overseas of an American Expeditionary Force.

It was not merely the power issue nor even the issue of national dignity that provided the driving force. It was the growing American conviction that there was a danger to the American way of life in the triumph of a government like that of imperial Germany. The American people had become more and more convinced that there was far more in common between them and the British and French than there was between them and the Germans. They were stirred by the invasion of Belgium, by the devastation of France, by the public bad manners of the German government (bad manners that long before 1914 had been an expensive luxury for the Germans). It is sometimes said or was sometimes written that the Germans lost their propaganda battle because the British cut the cables to America and the Germans could not tell their own story. But even in 1914 the wireless system existed and it was quite possible for the Germans to tell their own story, not only directly to America by air but indirectly through the American correspondents in Germany, through men like Karl Wiegand, and through other visitors to and admirers of the efficiency of the German army and state like Joseph M. Patterson, then of the *Chicago Tribune* and now of the New York *Daily News*. What cramped the style of German propagandists like George Sylvester Viereck in 1914 and 1939-41 was the awkward fact that the British agents, with all their cunning and unscrupulousness, were telling the truth—and of course embroidering it. What explained the trend of American opinion was not that there were certain difficulties in making clear why the Germans had to invade Belgium and sink the *Lusitania*. It was the fact that the Germans had invaded Belgium and sunk the *Lusitania*. If the German propaganda offices in Berlin had been able to denounce the reports of the burning of the Louvain Library and the destruction of Rheims Cathedral as lies made up out of whole cloth, that would have been something, just as their stout denial of having sunk the *Athenia* in 1939 was something—at least, for those resolved to believe anything.

It is not impossible that the world would have been better off, that there would have been an effectual exploitation of the victory of 1918 to secure peace for several generations (an aim that would have seemed preposterously impracticable to most of the human race a century ago), if the case for American intervention in 1917 had been represented in less moralistic terms. As it was, the American people saw themselves as giving—giving food and munitions and men to a general cause in which all the other peoples had material ends and the American people, alone, had purely moral ends in view. It was an attitude expressed in the words of a great man who was not sufficiently self-critical or critical of the aims of his own people. "Sometimes people call me an idealist. Well, that is the way I know I am an American. America is the only idealist nation in the world." So spoke Woodrow Wilson. It was not a very helpful attitude to bring to the solution of the problems of a world in which other people were as idealistic as they could afford to be, even if they could afford less idealism than Uncle Sam could. And only a nation giving constant proof of altruistic idealism could possibly have got away with this attitude of high moral superiority. No nation, not even the American nation, can keep at this high level all the time. So Europe was ironical at the expense of America, and America was shocked by the sight of Europe.

It might have been better if the Americans had had less high moral hopes at the beginning and, with a strong admixture of Yankee practicality, had compromised, openly, with the Mammon of Unrighteousness, taking this sinful world and the so-called human race more as they are and less as they should be, noting that men were made a little less than the angels, but did not stay at that high level.

There was a mutual disillusionment. Europe, which had hoped for a new birth of freedom, resented sermons from the United States of Harding and Coolidge. America, which had rightly seen herself as a liberator, was not ready enough to see that a real liberation had taken place and that there were possibilities in the Europe of Versailles if it could be integrated into a world system.

It is unnecessary to go into the long tragicomedy of disillusionment and recrimination. The intellectuals on both sides of the Atlantic had so much to say for Germany and so little to say about Germany and her neighbors that the man in the street was embittered or bored. Being less sentimental and less optimistic than his intellectual betters, the American man-in-the-street saw, from the beginning, that the only way to stop Hitler was to stop him—and the sooner the better. From 1933 on, it was a case for the sheriff or a vigilante committee, not for discussions as to why bandits turn bandits. The feebleness of the western European powers in those years justified any form of American contempt and, indeed, of American resentment. It was true that it was American aid that gave the Allies decisive victory in 1918. Why were the fruits of that victory let go so easily? Why were the Nazis allowed to begin with successful petty crime like stealing apples and confronted only with sermons? If this was all right, what had the last war been about? I have heard a distinguished American ask this question of a very distinguished Englishman who had nothing but the usual baloney about Versailles, etc., to offer. It was not good enough—as that Englishman learned before his death, when he had to fight an attitude of mind in America that he had helped to justify.

The Americans who asserted that America had been duped in 1917 did not need to use either German or American arguments; they had only to listen to the speeches, read the writings, and—still more—inspect the conduct of the rulers and leaders of France and Britain. But of course these last had plenty of help from Americans. Scholars, sciolists, charlatans, mercenaries, all combined to darken counsel. Moral optimism about Germany combined with moral pessimism about Britain to induce a more or less contemptuous resignation. Many complicated questions of historical responsibility were settled out-of-hand, and men famous for their vigilance in domestic matters were remarkably credulous outside the ring-fence of American territory. They were optimistic because they greatly underestimated the difficulties and, still more, the cost of keeping that fence in repair; they greatly underestimated the power of the nations that had designs on the fence and on what it enclosed. They extended their own view of the world too easily to other peoples. So one, the most eminent of all, thought that *All Quiet on the Western Front* was a German film—which not only was unjust to Hollywood, but had the consequence as well that too little attention was paid to the films that UFA and Hugenburg were providing for the German people, and too little attention also to what the German people were reading besides *All Quiet on the Western Front*. And really, if you classify *Carnival in Flanders* (*La Kermesse héroïque*) as a film showing the unattractiveness of war, your judgment of general human nature has been distorted to the point that limits your usefulness as a publicist.

◇◇◇◇◇◇◇◇◇◇

6

MAN DOES NOT live by bread alone, even pre-sliced bread, and the material optimism bred by American experience has not been accompanied by an equally incontestable spiritual self-confidence. Americans are men and women, subject to the strains and ordeals of humanity and they have, besides, inherited from Europe a cultural tradition that fights against mere naïve confidence in a world that, every day and in every way, gets better and better. Nevertheless, the American tradition is tied to the idea of progress. It has grown during the centuries in which that novel and revolutionary idea took possession of man's mind in the West, and all American experience has seemed to confirm the view that the world is advancing towards something better, to a fuller, richer life for more people, more of the time. What a great English scholar has written of the Dark Ages, out of which modern Europe and modern America have emerged, is almost comically unlike America. "If that age was an age of faith, it was not merely on account of its external religious profession; still less does it mean that the men of that age were more moral or more humane or more just in their social and economic relations than the men of today. It is rather because they had no faith in themselves or in the possibilities of human effort, but put their trust in something more than civilization and something outside history." *

The American historical experience has been totally different. It has been the product of profound faith in man's possibilities and of repeated historical justification for that faith. It is true that the

* Christopher Dawson: *The Making of Europe.*

[65]

religious tradition imported from Europe by the earlier settlers, especially in New England, had its ingredient of Christian humility and pessimism. President Eliot of Harvard, in the confident nineteenth century, was proclaiming an old New England attitude when he altered the inscription over the door of the new philosophy building in Harvard from "Man is the measure of all things," chosen by the philosophers, to "What is man that Thou art mindful of him?" chosen by himself. But even President Eliot was full of American optimism, as was made plain when in the person of George Santayana he encountered a representative of genuine Mediterranean pessimistic clarity. Another Eliot, in a later generation, was to take rather the side of Santayana than that of Charles Eliot, but Mr. T. S. Eliot, in choosing to live in England rather than in St. Louis or Boston, passed judgment not only on the American scene but indeed on his own fitness to adorn it.

Even in early New England, as Professor Perry Miller has shown, optimism about the destiny of man and society was always breaking in. The New England Calvinists of the first generation of Massachusetts and Harvard were, by the rigorous standards of sixteenth-century Calvinism, deplorably lax—not quite Arminian, but not really orthodox either. The American experience fought against the orthodox doctrine of Protestant Europe. When Jonathan Edwards in eighteenth-century Massachusetts tried to turn back the tide, he was defeated not merely because of his tactless investigation into the reading habits and the free conversation of the sons and daughters of the best families of Northampton, but because the campaign had already been lost. It was not even a rearguard action that he was fighting; it was a return from Elba for the old orthodoxy, a return that ended with a decisive Waterloo.

American religion was committed, more and more, to an optimistic view of God's purpose in the world and to an identification of that purpose with the purpose of man, especially American man. Religion more and more lost its supernatural and other-world character. God was conceived of as a kind of King of Brobdingnag convinced that "whoever could make two ears of corn, or two blades of grass, to grow upon a spot of ground where only one grew before, would deserve better of mankind, and do more essential service to his country, than the whole race of politicians put together." And not only than politicians but than unproductive saints. The American religious mind was made ready for the acceptance of the optimistic deism of Franklin and Jefferson, and thousands who would have been horrified to admit that they shared the religious views of those great heretics did in fact share more of their views than they suspected and were further removed from the views of old orthodox Christianity than they realized. The evangelical denominations might still insist on faith before works, but faith was expected to show forth its fruits in works, especially in economic works like abstention from extravagant vices like drink and sexual sin; greed or acquisitiveness was not only not condemned but more and more became a virtue.

It is no new opinion that since the Reformation there has been a more open identification of worldly prosperity with virtue than was openly preached if not practiced before. The virtues inculcated by evangelical religion bore fruit in wealth that was accepted as a proof of virtue. So far the American experience does not differ from the English. But the American experience has gone further. In some popular versions of modern American religion, prosperity is not merely evidence of virtue—it *is* virtue. It is no mere matter of seeking first the Kingdom of God and having wealth added unto you. Wealth, material success, happiness in this world *is* the Kingdom of God. If a reader doubts this let him read the literature issued from Moscow, Idaho, by Dr. Frank B. Robinson,* or "The [late] Great I Am," or

* See Dr. Robinson's advertisement in *The World Almanac* for 1943:

" 'I TALKED WITH GOD' " (Yes I Did—Actually and Literally) and as a result of that little talk with God, a strange Power came into my life. After 42 years of horrible, dismal, sickening failure, everything took on a brighter hue. It's fascinating to talk with God, and it can be done very easily, once you learn the secret. And when you do—well—there will come into your life the same dynamic Power which came into mine. The shackles of defeat which bound me for years went a-shimmering—and now?—well, I am President of the News Review Publishing Company, which corporation publishes the largest circulating afternoon daily in North Idaho. I own the largest office building in our City, I drive a beautiful Cadillac limousine. I own my own home, which has a lovely pipe-organ in it, and my family are abundantly provided for after I'm gone. And all this has been made possible because, one day, ten years ago, I actually and literally talked with God.

"You, too, may experience that strange mystical Power which comes from talking with God, and when you do, if there is poverty, unrest, unhappiness, listen to Father Divine, or con the advertising pages of the press of that great religious center, Los Angeles. What the early Christians promised for the next world, what other great religions have tried to persuade their adherents to despise, is for many Americans (in this possibly just one jump ahead of the English) the aim of religion. And Christian Science, in a less naïve way, represents the same refusal to accept the grim view of life that so many hundreds of generations of experience had made second nature to the human race. The optimism of poets like Shelley, their belief that

"the world's great age begins anew,"

was, after all, tempered by a fear that it might turn out to be another historical confidence trick.

"The world is weary of the past,
O might it die or rest at last."

Such pessimism was of course not at all unknown to Americans, to great Americans. It was Thoreau who observed with justice that most men live lives of "quiet desperation." It was the author of *Huckleberry Finn* who wrote *The Man That Corrupted Hadleyburg*. It was the American on whose life and example most hagiographical talent has been expanded, whose favorite poem began:

"O why should the spirit of mortal be proud?"

And it was again Lincoln who, after the fall of Richmond—when it was obvious that the Civil War was drawing to a triumphant close, that, as Whitman was to write:

"our fearful trip is done,
The ship has weathered every rack, the prize we sought is won"—

---

or ill-health in your life, well—this same God-Power is able to do for you what it did for me. No matter how useless or helpless your life seems to be—all this can be changed. For this is not a human Power I'm talking about—it's a God-Power. And there can be no limitations to the God-Power, can there?"

For one cent spent on a postal card, this secret will be revealed to anybody —or, at least, the first and cheapest steps can be taken. The present population of Moscow, Idaho, is 6,000, a rise of nearly 2,000 in ten years, much of which may well be due to the business brought by Dr. Robinson. The circulation figures for *The Daily Idahonian* are not given in *The Editor and Publisher*. But the biggest paper in the state has just 20,000, so Dr. Robinson is a booster as well as a mystic.

made no such triumphant comment, but repeated, with all his melancholy emphasis, a very different passage of poetry:

> *"Duncan is in his grave;*
> *After life's fitful fever he sleeps well;*
> *Treason has done his worst; nor steel, nor poison,*
> *Malice domestic, foreign levy, nothing,*
> *Can touch him further."*

But the American tradition most effectively publicized is not disposed to worry over

> *"the dead,*
> *Whom we to gain our peace, have sent to peace."*

That life is not reducible to formulas, that there are bound to be sorrows and disillusionment even for the best prepared, for the new elect who have had the right eugenic ancestry, the proper education, the necessary contacts—these ideas are heresy in modern America. The man who has cured himself of B.O. and halitosis, has learned French to surprise the waiter and the saxophone to amuse the company, may, as Heywood Broun said, find that people still avoid him because they do not like him.

But is it a heresy entertained by a few cranks only, or in fact half-believed in by a great part of the population? In a country where it is news, comforting news, that "Life begins at forty," some scepticism must have crept into the national viewpoint. Some people must have been thinking that life comes to an end when the first illusions, the first hopes, the fresh power of youth, are exhausted, that American life is designed for boys and young men, for girls of course, too, but not for adults. If this belief is or was widespread, one reason is to be found (as critical Americans have pointed out) in a view of life in which success is identified with competitive success—not with attaining a fixed standard, but with winning a place in the first ten of every hundred. As far as this view *is* accepted, it condemns the vast majority to failure, since ninety per cent must be ranked as unsuccessful. It is true that the man who is successful in one line may be unsuccessful in all others—and much American advertising is devoted to making some man anxious about his appearance, his fluency in speech, even his smell, who yet has valid economic or professional grounds for complacency. On the other hand, the man who is unsuccessful in his business or profession can find some compensation through buying culture or some other non-priceable good. He can be induced to look forward to a secure old age by an insurance company, or to a new and vigorous middle age by the advertisers of religions, education, body-belts, or what-have-you. But the American man-in-the-street is descended not from buyers of wooden nutmegs, but from sellers of them. He takes advertising seriously, but not so seriously as all that. He is not surprised to learn from Mr. John R. Tunis that the economic record of a Harvard "class," twenty years on, makes depressing reading—if from a higher education a large cash income is anticipated. He remembers catastrophes like that of 1929, following which the current hotel joke was the question put by the clerk: "What do you want a room for—sleeping in, or jumping from?" The anxieties of the American business man, his needs for health farms, like the need of his wife for psychoanalysis and yoga, make another standard national joke. The fresh, boyish, unlined, happy and, in the good sense of the term, ingenuous faces of the young American soldiers whom one can see in the London Underground, are replaced in twenty years' time by faces as marked by "the contagion of the world's slow stain" as those of the sharp-faced, acute, cynical Cockney soldiers are, if not from birth at least from adolescence. The world cannot be made safe for boys and girls, no matter how hard parents and society may try. They do grow up—and if they don't, the worse for them.

It is perhaps the competitive strain of American life that accounts for the excessive gloom of current American letters. Just as an American advertiser is not content, like his English colleague, to tell you that "XXX is good for you," but insists that "XXX is better," on sale at the "better" bars or five-and-tens, the American novelist insists on telling you that things are worse and getting worse all the time. A great deal of this literary pessimism is mere fashion; the black paint is shot on by a paint-gun in the literary assembly line. In most cases it is merely Eddie Guest and Harold Bell Wright in reverse. But in the case of the better writers it is more than that: it is a resentful criticism of American life as being full of promises that no society

can, in fact, keep. It is not valid criticism of modern American literature that it takes a gloomy view, that it shows the unhappy side of
American life. If it does, if it is bitterly critical, that is no novelty; so
were many admitted past masters: Howells in his political novels,
Henry James in his life, the western agrarians of 1900 in their gritty
pictures of life on the farm or in the small Kansas or Nebraska town.
If Aldous Huxley is right in attributing German inability to handle
the problem of modern personal life to the rarity of good German
novels, Americans ought to be grateful to their novelists who provide
them with abundant precedents for all possible emergencies. And it
would be a fraud on the public not to provide a sufficient number
of ugly, awkward, dangerous, and painful situations, for we shall
none of us miss experiences of that type. A happy literature is a
dangerous drug.

But the pessimistic American writers, from Dreiser to Mary Mc-
Carthy, have, in fact, helped to break down the American view of
life into still unreconciled attitudes. The optimistic religion of business and progress proved inadequate, and with its collapse other parts
of the national religion were at least shaken. The standards of family
morals, of sexual behavior, were affected. It is true that a great deal
of the alarm over the dangerous immorality of modern American letters was silly. The book censors who hunted for improper words were
no better employed than the beach or movie censors who measured
bathing suits with an inch tape or sweaters with the eyes of a lubri-
cious geometrician. Nevertheless, the censors, however stupid, were
vaguely registering a great change, the invasion of sexual morals by
the competitive standard that had conquered business.

Advertising and fiction alike told boys and girls that sexual happiness was theirs on pretty reasonable terms. Mr. James J. Walker was
wrong when he said that "no girl had ever been ruined by a book,"
though he was right in thinking that no girl would be saved by idiotic
censorship, especially if it left advertising sections alone, as being
business and not art. For literature and advertising both presented
possible lines of conduct that had been "unthinkable" (though, of
course, thought of) a generation before. They offered precedents for
action that came home to the young and produced more strains, more
differences between the fiction of American life and the fact. And

as another unsuccessful municipal politician could have told ex-Mayor Walker, it was nothing new:

> *"Galeotto fu il libro e chi lo scrisse:*
> *Quel giorno più non vi leggemo avanti."*

Again, what was mere nonsense for boys and girls, whatever ethical dangers it involved, was dangerous for adults, for either it bred in them an easy optimism, the view that the shortest way across was the best way round; or it bred a premature pessimism and added to the amount of dissent from the official Panglossian religion that all was for the best in the best of all possible republics—or would be as soon as That Man was out of the White House. More people than was really necessary reacted, reacted by divorce, by neurosis, by an affected gloom that was no more impressive or convincing than so much real estate optimism. And it was not a moment too soon that one of the acutest American sociologists issued his manifesto called *Let Your Mind Alone*.

But literary pessimism was not merely pessimism about this "so-called human race," merely doubts about "how to tell man from the apes." It was pessimism about that part of American life which had, historically, best justified American optimism—American economic prospects.

Literary pessimism about American life was not an invention of the twenties. Around 1900, the long depression years had had their reflection in regional novels that described, with depressing fidelity, what it was like to live in Ed Howe's Kansas or Hamlin Garland's "Middle Border." But for all their sincerity, for all the gritty verisimilitude of their style, the prairie novelists did not seem to get to grips with any general human problems. Of all the ills their heroes and heroines had to endure, there seemed to be few that dollar wheat wouldn't have cured. A much better novelist, Howells, was driven to writing socialist novels of the future by anger at the American present. Jack London predicted the rise of fascism, and there were plenty of literary spokesmen for the age of Wilson's "New Freedom." The "novel of social significance" was not new when it became the rage in the thirties.

But what *was* new was the general agreement among the new leisure class created by the new American economy—the women, and the sons of the successful pioneers—that life in Gopher Prairie, in Zenith, in New York, even in Paris, was hard to live. That pessimism was often affected and not of the highest quality. Indeed, the classic of this age, *Babbitt*, was not a pessimistic book at all, for George F. Babbitt survives his soul-killing experiences as a human being who would not have been improved in any sense of the term by living in the Rue de la Huchette.

On top of this literary pessimism came the genuine pessimism bred by the depression. Here the writers were representing a general national mood and one which still colors much of American life. For behind a good deal of optimism is the memory of the great collapse, and behind a good deal of apparently thoughtless determination to have the best of both worlds in war and in peace is the terrifying memory of the years in which the American dream seemed to have become a nightmare: a nightmare of unemployment, of bankruptcy, bankruptcy of individuals, of great corporations, of cities, of states, an age of the destruction of normal economic expectation, the most fatal failure of a capitalist society. No novels or plays could exaggerate the indignation, the shock felt by millions of Americans at the coming not of hard times, but of a general collapse of leadership, a general betrayal of confidence. "Sez you" became the cry of millions who had been well-behaved, credulous, good citizens, dutifully keeping both feet on the ground—only to find the ground giving way under them.

This was reflected in literature, in plays, even in films. It was reflected but exaggerated. There was a sudden wave of literary revolutionary affectation. Communism was pretty nearly the only wear and a very high proportion of young American writers either passed through the party ranks or were "fellow-travelers." A few stayed. It was the time in which a reportage of fairly normal labor riots and strike incidents could be solemnly published under the title *America Faces the Barricades*. It was the incubation period of the New Deal.

There were external reasons why this literary extremism did not last. The control of the American Communist party was not much more intelligent than that of any other Comintern branch, but the American heretics and schismatics were not like their timid English brethren, content to go into the garden and eat worms or dirt. They spoke up in meeting. They denounced and deplored and, in the old tradition of the mourners' bench at a frontier camp meeting, confessed their own sins and the sins of the unrepentant. There were half a dozen heresies apart from the great Trotskyist schism.

And with the first turn of the tide in 1933, the revolutionary temper of the American people turned out to have been a case of wrong diagnosis. It was only depression measles. It was no longer "Farewell to Reform" but Goodbye to Revolution. The revolutionary intelligentsia scattered in all directions—some into the New Deal, some into pure letters, some into pessimistic conservatism, at least one into the embraces of the Dies Committee set up to smell out communism with the zeal and technique of a witch-doctor at work in a kraal in darkest Africa.

The pessimists were replaced by the far more interesting preachers of historical optimism. And that optimism (a sign of the times) was based on the American past as well as on the American future. There was a cultivation of literary archeology; a change from little periodicals on the Left Bank to forgotten Southern and New England masters. Historical novels, historical films, primitive American art, primitive American thought, were given a new value by the need for restoring American self-esteem as well as by the spectacle of Hitler's Europe or the Russia of the great purge.

The movement was, up to a point, healthy. It was better than precious imitations of European preciosity. But it was forced to ignore too many truths to be wholly healthy. Early American art was interesting, but it was not much more than that. Where it was most successful was in the adaptation of European models, in Richmond or Charleston or Salem. There were admirable architects and craftsmen in eighteenth-century America, but that was all. Gilbert Stuart is a good painter, but he does not compare very well with his contemporary, Goya. Shaker craftsmanship was sound, but a Shaker village did not compare very well with Fountains Abbey or La Chaise Dieu. For all that Mr. Van Wyck Brooks or Miss Constance Rourke could do, the American record in these fields of achievement was mediocre.

There was more to be said for a cultivation of really primitive art, of American folklore. But again, there was too much forcing of the issue. The Americans were the heirs of English, Scottish, Irish folk song but they did not increase their inheritance or improve it. *Frankie and Johnny* is an amusing ballad, but it is not *Helen of Kirkconnel*. Perhaps, as an eminent authority has hinted, the numerous unprinted folk songs do the American genius more credit; but even in this field there is no great originality and there are still importations from the old world like *John Glaister*. As far as the man-in-the-street is concerned, the situation was further complicated by the synthetic character of much of the folk song he hears and likes and thinks of as deeply and traditionally American. Primitive art that is not really primitive is boring in the not very long run. When on a vaudeville circuit a modern cowboy asks with false naïveté whether the stars he sees are "big peopled worlds like our own," he is competing not with genuine folk song but with Leopardi. He cannot long stand the competition of:

> "*a che vale*
> *Al pastor la sua vita,*
> *La vostra vita a voi?*"

When a nation is at such a stage of sophistication as the Americans have reached, it is idle to try to fob them off with songs their mothers would have sung to them if the industry had been as well organized as it is now. All that the modern ballad-makers can do was better done by Stephen Foster than it is ever done today.

So we have to fall back on the real artists, on the men and women who are willing to follow their spirit where it listeth. And it is hard to discriminate, hard for the critic and hard for the common reader. Even the toughness and brutality, the crudity of language may become as much of a convention as the prudery of a generation ago. Mr. Cole Porter has truly asserted:

> "*Good authors, too, who once knew better words,*
> *Now only use four-letter words, writing prose*
> *Anything goes.*"

But there was a great deal to be said, too, for the young woman who remarked: "Oh, I never thought anybody *said* those things. I thought they only appeared in books!"

This is not the place (or it would be as easy as it is tempting) to praise contemporary American literature, so abundant, so varied, so courageous, so entertaining, so much the senior partner now in the English-speaking world. But it has not yet done what is necessary for national unification. It has not provided what Mr. G. M. Young rightly credited Mr. H. G. Wells with providing a generation ago in England, a new *Cortegiano*, a picture and standard of the modern world that neither crushed energy and optimism nor was so sugar-coated and irrelevant as to drive the young off in angry derision.

7

IN AMERICA the role of the farmer has been almost as important historically as it has been emotionally. The land that was settled, cleared, tilled has been the creation of the farmer, in most areas a creation that is quite recent in time. In Europe the basic work was done hundreds, even thousands, of years ago; some historians may recall the primitive settlers, the makers of the first efficient plows, or such restorers of material and spiritual culture as the monks of Monte Cassino. But all that is remote. In America there are many men still alive who remember that last great western push of settlement on to the great plains. Settlement in the cut-over timber lands of northern Minnesota or Wisconsin is quite recent. Even regions that had seemed to be doomed to total abandonment like Vermont have had a new lease of life as milk producers. A high proportion of the immigrants who have settled on marginal abandoned lands—like the Poles in Wisconsin or in the tobacco lands of the Connecticut Valley—have preserved, for one generation at least, the peasant attitude of reverence for the soil. Americans who have migrated to the city from the countryside or the small country town have inherited many rural habits of mind. And the rural bias of the American people has been reinforced by a political system that overweighs the rural vote in federal and still more in state elections, and by a historical tradition that has been adequate for a farmers' republic, for the egalitarian, free, rural democracy of Jefferson and Jackson. For an American, therefore, even if he is a city dweller, there is something especially outrageous in the long decline in relative economic importance and in social stability of the American farm population. That less than half of the American population should now live in rural areas, that only a quarter of the population should be living on farms—this is novel, disconcerting, improper. And the American farmer is more or less consciously exploiting a situation in which his own natural desire to get a "reasonable" share in the total national income is politically supported by not very clear-minded town dwellers, as well as by quite clear-minded statesmen and sociologists who hold that a contented and numerous rural population is a necessity for a healthy republic.

It would be unrealistic to underestimate the power of this rural bias. The conquest of the United States by the plow has been the most generally approved American victory. It is only today that critical experts are beginning to wonder whether the plow has not been an enemy of the American land and, more confidently, to ask is American policy to be devoted to keeping a large population employed at a low economic level on the land or to producing from that land the largest quantities of needed crops? Such scepticism has to fight a centuries-old national tradition that makes of the advancing farmer the great folk hero. Not until the independent settlers had made the forest, then the prairie, then the High Plains, into plowland, was the great American folk-movement over. The ballads of the nation fight the figures of the agronomists. So far the ballads have it.

For the winning of the West, the making of all America, bred its legends, not only the legends of the great pathfinders or great Indian fighters, but of the bringers of the gifts of civilization. There was the legend of Johnny Appleseed, that John Chapman who carried his apples all over the West, most famous of those who

> In the days of President Washington,
> The glory of the nations,
> Dust and ashes,
> Snow and sleet,
> And hay and oats and wheat,
> Blew west,
> Crossed the Appalachians.*

And with the wheat and the hay and the apples came civilization:

> A ballot-box in each apple,
> A state capital in each apple,
> Great high schools, great colleges,
> All America in each apple.*

Americans like Johnny Appleseed, like the bold South Carolina woman who introduced indigo culture, like John Rolfe who did more for the future by curing Virginia tobacco than by marrying Pocahontas, like Edmund Ruffin who found the way to restore the wasted lands of tide-water Virginia, like a hundred plant-and-cattle breeders —these were the American equivalents of Pallas and Flora and the other Greek and Roman benefactors of the husbandman. To the prairie farmer's clever son, the *Georgics* were the most relevant Latin poetry—and one clever daughter of a pioneer professor has told us what Virgil meant to her in raw Nebraska. Miss Willa Cather, who has combined the *Eclogues* and the *Georgics* in *My Ántonia,* is only the most accomplished prose Virgil of the great settlement.

The corn, the maize higher than a man's head, was the oldest and most representative American crop. "Down where the tall corn grows" was a true folk song and the annual corn-husking championship was the true Olympic festival of a farmer people. It is probably pure sentiment to regret the passing of the tall corn; in some regions, at least, it is profitably replaced by shorter and more useful and economical though less impressive corn plants. The great combines on the west-

* Quoted by permission of the publisher from *Collected Poems of Vachel Lindsay* (New York: The Macmillan Co., 1925).

ern plains, as well as other labor-saving devices, have reduced to a mere battalion the once great army of migratory harvesters who, under the derogatory title of "hoboes" or the even more dangerous epithet of "Wobblies," moved from state to state with the harvest. Their songs are going too:

> *"You advertise in Omaha,*
> *'Come, leave the valley of the Kaw.'*
> *Nebraska calls, 'Don't be misled,*
> *We'll furnish you a feather bed!' "*

But the Rock Candy mountains of the hoboes, like the revolutionary dreams of the I.W.W. (the Wobblies), have passed beyond the horizon as the American farmer has adjusted himself slowly and reluctantly to a new mechanical world in which the old laws seem to have been replaced.

First of all, the American farmer's share in the national income has not only fallen as the proportion of farmers to the total population has fallen; it has fallen even lower than mere proportions would suggest. The farmers, as a class, have undergone all the downward pressures of American life in the period between the two wars, but they have only in a slight degree benefited by the boom times. During the last war, the farmer, like everybody else, got a greatly increased cash income (though not nearly so much as he thought he should have got; price fixing was as unpopular then as now—as the Democratic administration learned at the 1920 elections). There was a general discounting of a rise in the value of farm land that had doubled the amount of agricultural mortgages between 1910 and 1920. But the farm income, which in 1919 was $17,000,000,000 odd, fell catastrophically; and even when good times had returned for industry, it was only $12,000,000,000 in 1926. When the great collapse of 1929-33 began, it was again the farmers who took the worst rap. Farm income in 1931 was less than a third of farm income in 1919.

It was no wonder that the American farmer, his whole security endangered, his whole normal expectation of profit made ludicrous, should have been embittered, angry against all the forces, occult and open, that seemed to make sure that he always got the wrong end of the bargain. He was not prepared (who would have been?) to accept the fact that the tide of economic development had turned against him. For instance, the Midwest farmer's basic problem was to decide in any given year whether to feed his corn crop to his pigs and sell the pigs, or to cut down his pig production and sell his corn. The majority of farmers were sure to guess wrong. For if the majority bred pigs, pigs were cheap and corn dear; and if, next year, the majority sold corn and neglected pigs, pigs were dear and corn cheap. To play the game against the "corn-hog" cycle required foresight, respect for statistics, and either a successful determination not to do what your neighbors did, or a highly organized system of coöperative marketing and production. For the majority, whose decision was the main price determinant, only the second solution was open. And the American farmer was highly individualistic, a slow and sceptical coöperator, always ready to take a chance to beat the market—a state of mind bred in him by political and social institutions and by a highly variable climate. For a catastrophe that destroyed crops in one region might have no effect in another which would benefit by the short supply. Farming was a gamble and that was the way the American farmer liked it.

It was natural, too, that the farmer should have looked out for foreign as well as for domestic devils. Though he did not really appreciate it, his competitive power in the overseas markets was being weakened. For one thing, with the development of ground-nuts in West Africa, the slow, indirect way of producing fats through lard was made expensive. Indeed, the cottonseed oil of the South was a dangerous competitor of Iowa lard *inside* the American tariff wall. And that wall made it harder for the potential customers of the American farmer to buy what he had to sell—in direct competition with Canada, Australia, and Argentina and in indirect competition with all the subtropical products made available by modern technology and made additionally formidable competitors by changes in dietary habits.

For two generations, the American farmer by voting the Republican ticket and supporting a high tariff policy had shown notable disinterestedness, if cloudy economic thinking, for he thus helped to pay the high price of industrializing America. By the 1920's, he was still voting the Republican ticket and supporting very high tariffs indeed, but he was no longer content to let it go at that. He knew that protection for his basic crops was superfluous; what he wanted was a share in the total national income proportional to his numbers (which could be computed) and to his social and political merits which were more open to dispute. So he supported schemes like the McNary-Haugen bill, which was the first serious attempt to use the taxing power of the Union to compensate the farmer for his tariff-induced losses. But it was now questionable whether the traditional roles had not been reversed and whether American industry, now interested in its export market, was not having to pay the costs of keeping alive American agriculture on a scale to which the nation was accustomed. The bean growers of Michigan could be protected against unfair foreign competition, but of what profit was that to the automobile industry of Michigan which needed markets, not protection? But the farmer (with a great deal of non-farm support) continued the attack, and the refusal of the Republican presidents to sanction such subsidies to the farm interest helped to produce that revulsion against the Grand Old Party which led millions of American farmers to vote in 1932 and in 1936 with no grateful regard for the fact that the Republican party had saved the Union two generations or more before.

But the prices of crops were not the only worry of the farmer or of the nation. The very existence of the land was at stake over wide regions. The explorers of the early nineteenth century had marked the region west of the Missouri "the great American desert." It was roughly all the land west of 100°; it was marked by the change in its rainfall and in its vegetable cover. East of 100° was the tall-grass country that got the necessary twenty inches of rain a year; west was the short-grass country that could not rely on the necessary rainfall, a region in which the native grasses were hammered into a moisture-holding mat by the feet of the millions of buffalo and totally undisturbed by the nomadic Indians who lived off the buffalo. But as the tide of settlement moved west, these lands designed for buffalo and then for cattle were coveted by the would-be settlers brought in, with their new plows and reapers, by the new railroads.

A series of exceptionally wet years made the fears of the geographers seem folly or treason. There were some individual catastrophes. There was the famous story of the pioneers who had set out for the

West with the legend painted on their wagon "Pike's Peak or Bust," and who came back with the legend revised to "Pike's Peak and Busted." There was the story of the westward-moving optimist who met the eastward-moving pessimist. "This would be a fine country if it had water." "So would Hell!"

But not until the end of the eighties was there a serious recession of settlement in western Kansas and Nebraska and in the Dakotas. There are counties in those states whose population has never been so high as it was in the census of 1890. It was discovered that there *were* limits to settlement; that the rainfall was often inadequate; that the belief that plowing itself increased the rainfall was a booster's error, made in more or less good faith.

The economic equilibrium established round 1900 was badly upset by the first World War. The demand for wheat was immense; prices were high; more and more land was plowed up, including land that should never have been plowed. All the post-war sorrows of the American farmer fell with especial weight on the shoulders of the farmer on the new western frontier between the well-watered and the semi-arid lands. Low prices hit him worst; he had fewest capital resources; he was farthest from domestic markets; was most at the mercy of world prices as recorded in the Chicago wheat pit or in Winnipeg or Liverpool. In these states the radical political movements—Farmer-Labor parties, the Nonpartisan League, radical dissent within the Democratic party in the southern section, in Oklahoma and Texas—upset the old political system. There was a return to the spirit of the insurgent nineties when Mrs. Lease, the "Kansas Pythoness," advised her fellow-citizens "to raise less corn and more hell." Old established radical dynasties like the La Follettes; new figures like Governor Floyd Olson in Minnesota and Senator Nye and Governor Langer in North Dakota, returning figures from the past like "Alfalfa Bill" Murray in Oklahoma, expressed this discontent with an economic system that was a purely negative lottery: all blanks and no prizes.

But the worst times came with the general depression, with the general collapse of rural credit, with the foreclosures on a great scale that marked the collapse of farm values and, even in so rich, well-farmed, and well-ordered a state as Iowa, led to something like a *jacquerie*. Far worse was the situation of the High Plains farmer. For nature took a hand and inflicted a series of catastrophic droughts, droughts which got the attention of the most urban-minded Americans. For the dry, loose soil of the marginal farms simply blew into the air. Hundreds of miles away in Minneapolis, the soil from Dakota farms piled up on the carpets of the houses, and over a thousand miles away it darkened the sky in New York. Away to the South, in western Texas and Oklahoma, it was a case of farm lands turning to sand; and the poor, ill-educated, ill-equipped marginal farmers there began that long, uninspiring trek westward to California. The "Okies" of *The Grapes of Wrath* were a novelty in American history, mostly defeated, dispirited fugitives from soil that had been opened to settlement only in 1890 and was desert by 1934.

Farther north, things were not quite so bad. The Scandinavian farmers of the Dakotas had more technical resources and more capital. Even in the worst year of all, 1934—when the rolling country west of the Missouri looked, at a distance, like a Scottish moor covered with a kind of heather that was, in fact, wheat stunted to a few inches by the drought, when the dying cattle were shipped hundreds of miles east by the federal government to water—there was no despair. "A good year will set us all right," a Swedish farmer told me when I spoke of the theory that arable farming would have to be abandoned altogether. And an Irish settler, a veteran a hundred miles farther west, said this was bad, but not so bad as the grasshopper year in the seventies when he had brought horses up from Nebraska and could not water them for three days because every water-hole was full of dead "locusts."

But no amount of courage could make it less of a disaster. The whole credit structure collapsed. Such exhibitions of state pride as the skyscraper capitol of North Dakota that soars out of the plain at Bismarck seemed doomed to be an American equivalent of the statue of Ozymandias. "They say we must pay our debts, but they tell you that they understand why you can't pay your war debts," said a Swedish farmer to me that year in the scorched country west of the Missouri. "If you can't pay, how can we? And our debts are just as much war debts as yours. We contracted them to raise crops for you. The government wouldn't let wheat prices rise, but it let them fall all right. We won't quit and we won't pay."

Even in less desolated regions, there was the same anger, the same sense of frustration, the same nostalgia for the good days before Europe went mad and the American land ceased to rise in value every decade and even ceased to stay put. For this last outrage of all, the blame was imputed to the East—and Europe is part of the East.

The American farmer and all American society had been taught for over three centuries to have a sacred respect for the land. This did not prevent its being exploited, mined rather than farmed; but trust in the American soil, the producer of good things, *magna parens frugum,* was as lively in American as in Roman breasts. That land, it must be remembered, had never known what Europe has so often known and Asia knows nearly all the time, the terror of a great famine. Many Americans have gone hungry in the past, some go hungry now; undernourishment as well as stupid nourishment is endemic in certain regions. But America has not gone through an experience like that of Ireland in 1846-47 or that of Ukraine a few years ago. To find the American soil revolting, refusing to bear, blowing away, having to be abandoned (in the case of Oklahoma only a generation after the first settlement), was the most disturbing sign of all those that pointed to a need for a national stocktaking. The decade between 1920 and 1930 was the first in American history (since the white man came) in which the forest area *increased*—and that meant less an intelligent replanting of cut-over land than the natural springing-up of scrub. To have to take thought for the morrow of the whole American land, this was a reminder that even the United States was not exempt from the general limitations of our human dwelling-place.

It has been a disillusioned, often embittered, and still more often puzzled farmer who has had to make the great reorientation to the war. The first job of making America was his; his were the hopes of most representative Americans. He found that America would not stay made, that Nature and unknown, remote, and evil forces still combined to thwart him. He was saved from expropriation by the "Triple A" programs of the first Roosevelt administration. For the moment he was grateful. "Landon won't carry a county west of here," said a prominent Republican in a Middle West state in my hearing in 1936; "Harry Wallace will carry them all."

But the Republican party (of which the speaker is a senatorial ornament) has come back all the same. For the farmer didn't like not growing crops, killing young pigs, adjusting his methods of farming not to his own guesses and hopes but to remote statistical calculations in Washington. As long as he had no other cash resources, the federal checks were gladly, even gratefully, received. But when he got a chance to make money again by growing as much as possible, he jumped at it. And then to learn that he had to submit to more rigorous controls, do without tractors sent to Britain or Russia, do without sons and hired hands sent to Guadalcanal or Iceland or Libya—this was to have another lesson in the perverseness of the nature of things and a new temptation to look for the devils who were in part, at least, responsible for this new disaster. One of those devils was of course Hitler; another and much more hated one was Tojo, or any representative Japanese; but others were Americans—above all the remote "bureaucrats" who didn't know the life of a dirt farmer and his needs and deserts.

Farmers have long supplied the soldiers for most societies. But in all countries farmers dislike war, however resigned they may be to it. Its waste seems to them (as it does to women) a contradiction of all the habits of normal, healthy, and beneficent life. And two wars in one generation, two wars not at all obviously connected with the needs of the farmer in the Great Valley, make a demand on critical imagination that cannot be met, at any rate in full. Patriotism, national pride, the acceptance of the legitimate authority of the United States, these are in many cases substitutes and adequate substitutes for that complete grasp of the ideological issues of the war that comes easily to editorial writers. Thinking his the most important national activity, convinced that all other forms of economic life are parasitic on his, the American farmer (or any farmer) is resigned to war but sceptical about its conduct. So he does not take kindly to economic controls; they are worse than the draft that takes his son. He knows the limits of planning (can *they* control the rainfall?). But it must be remembered that in the rural areas there is less opposition to this war than to the last one; there is a lot less than there was to the Civil War, in North and South alike. And the American farmer has got hold of one truth at last. "It takes more than one to keep the peace" is a more useful maxim than that "it takes two to make a quarrel."

And converting the farmer is very important indeed. For the American city does not reproduce itself. It used to live off immigration from Europe and the country; now it must live off immigration from the country, and in every American city and town a very large section of the population are still farm boys in sentiment, still in touch with the land, still half convinced that only farmers really know the answers.

Yet more than half of the American people now live in areas classified as "urban," and if some of those areas are urban only in a census-taker's mind, many residents in technically rural areas are really city dwellers. The devotee of the old New England rural life of Bronson Alcott's boyhood who sought it round Westport, Connecticut, would be wasting his time.

The new roads and the new cars, and the closer integration of national life that these have made possible, have led to a very rapid sophistication of the remaining rural population. Reuben, the hick farmer of vaudeville, is a fiction as dated as a Keystone Comedy. Even small country towns have been urbanized in appearance and in temper. Movies, advertising, mail-order houses, ease of travel have undermined the cracker-barrel on which the traditional rural philosopher sat. The last great effort to impose rural moral standards—Prohibition—failed, and legal puritanism now finds its political driving force in urban Catholicism, not in rural Protestantism. The pin-up girl, not booze, is the enemy to be extirpated by the arm of the law, and the dangerous seductions of *Esquire* are not burning topics in the corn belt.

The urbanization of the American country has followed fairly closely on the urbanization of the American city, on its coming-of-age, its acceptance of the facts that a city is not merely an overgrown village and that city life is a new way of life to be learned. And it is in the American cities, outside of New York and a few of the older eastern regional capitals, that the coming-of-age of the American way of life can be most easily seen.

The American cities were and are very unlike ours. There is no real capital; New York may be a playground for socially ambitious Westerners, or even for Bostonians or Philadelphians anxious to relax a little; but persons whose position on the Main Line or in Beacon Street is secure do not seek to climb to Fifth or later to Park Avenue. Distances are too great for social centralization, and the idea of Washington as a social center is older than the New Deal though not much. A city like Seattle, like Louisville, like Cleveland, like Milwaukee, has bred its own society, imposed its own standards, refusing scions of great Boston dynasties admission into the best brewing circles of Milwaukee, not taking too seriously the visitors to Louisville for whom it was merely the home of the Kentucky Derby.

The towns grew few or none of the English provincial-town complexes. They knew they were not so big as New York (the only American city that can afford to call itself *little* and *old*) or even Chicago, but they had their own standards, their own society. Mark Twain settled down in Hartford; Howells had doubts about quitting Boston for New York; so great a newspaperman as William Allen White stayed in Emporia all his days; and as for persuading a citizen of San Francisco that he would gain anything by moving elsewhere—why, confusing him or her with a mere "Angeleno" could hardly be more offensive! The cities, large and small, became more attractive as streets were paved, water brought in, capital spent on civic improvements. The days are long past when there was justification for the New York reporter who was sent to cover a fire in Rome, New York, and wired his office: "This town seems to have been built in a day."

For one thing, towns have become much cleaner, much more habitable. That adjustment of the American people to the American climate which modern wealth and technology have brought about has made the cities habitable in a way they were not a generation ago. Improved local transport, for instance, has abolished the horrors of the horse car in winter, the horrors that tested the moral fiber of Olive Chancellor in the Boston of the 1870's. No longer do pigs scavenge on Upper Broadway, and if Philadelphia's water supply is still very bad, the city does have a subway.

The dirt, untidiness, lack of unity of the American city were necessary aspects of its fantastic growth. No doubt corrupt municipal politics accounted for a good deal; so did the recent rural habits of most city dwellers. But it was, above all, a case of priorities. Not every thing would be done at once. The cities were too busy growing not to sprawl. It is obvious that the Baltimore of Mr. Mencken's and Cardinal Gibbons's boyhood must have been a charming place to live in, but on a hot day the smells must have detracted from the charm as they still do in places like East St. Louis. Mr. Booth Tarkington's Indianapolis; Tom Johnson's Cleveland; the Chicago of the early Dreiser, full of energy and civic pride—these also were primitive in a good many ways. Primitive, but not provincial.

The consequences are not merely agreeable for the city-dwellers, they are important for the world. For they encourage the regional feeling, the regional diversity of the American people. They make it almost as silly as ever to look to New York or Washington, or even to Chicago or Hollywood, to find out what the American people are thinking. Great areas may be thinking nothing; great areas may be thinking totally different things. "Almost as silly," for of course there has been a great deal of integration. Radio with its national star commentators and newscasters; the movies with their influence on the tastes of the multitude and their reflection of what high paid guessing experts think the public wants; the national columnists, syndicated in newspapers and magazines all over the country; the lecturers, telling the same tale from Sandusky to San Diego—all these have made it easier to estimate what the American people think or will think. But they have not made irrelevant the important truth that there are no provinces, no areas ready to take a lead from a center, no universally accepted body of makers and moulders of public opinion.

The great American cities have their own great newspapers, as the greatest British cities have. But there are hundreds of small city papers, too, some of which may be more important in their area than any metropolitan paper is in its. "I don't care what the London *Times* said of me—I'm waiting to see what the *Skibbereen Eagle* says." The Irish M.P. who was being epigrammatic in London would have been uttering the merest platitude in Washington.

The local magnate is not often thinking of how quickly he can get away to some region where his origin is little known and settle down as a country squire. It is true that once the connection with the grass-roots is cut, he may do just that; but if he does he loses all power and prestige in the region from which his fortune came.

More often he and others like him will be the founders or bene-factors of local museums like the admirable one in Seattle or the magnificent one in Kansas City. The local universities, state or private; the local municipal universities like those in Cincinnati or Louisville; new city universities like those in Detroit and Kansas City—these are centers of local pride, of local opinion, of local contro-versy. So are the local preachers and the local politicians.

Sometimes the prestige of the city outside its own region may be more or less accidental. It is certain that not many people would have heard of Rochester, Minnesota, if the Mayo brothers had not established their famous clinic in their home town. The New Yorkers had to come to them as other New Yorkers had to go to Reno. Rochester, New York, owes a good deal of its importance to the munificence of George Eastman who gave great endowments to the university, founded the great music school, and gave a subject to Mr. Paul Horgan for *The Fault of Angels*.

Literature reflects this healthy provincialism. Not only are there good regional novelists and poets but, odder still, there is no taboo on fictional crime outside New York and its neighborhood. Some of the best modern American crime stories are located round Duluth; Mr. Dashiell Hammett's hero practices in San Francisco; Perry Mason works inside the law in Los Angeles County; there are emi-nent fictional crime detectors at work as far apart as Dallas and Cape Cod.

There is a great professional orchestra in a city so geographically remote as Minneapolis, which also serves as the home town of the most admired American Shakespearean scholar, well over a thou-sand miles, both of them, from New York or the Folger Library in Washington.

It is this regional autonomy that justifies, as far as it can be justified, the locality rule in politics. The law that prohibits an American citizen from representing in Congress a state in which he does not live and, in effect, limits the members of the House of Representa-tives to men and women living in the actual districts concerned, is a serious handicap to Congress as an efficient maker of national policy. But how natural, how inevitable it is in the United States! The case of Canada shows that a large, federal country need not impose this self-denying ordinance on its voters; but once it has been imposed, how hard to get it repealed, in law or practice!

So it goes; the local radio stations, even if members of a chain, have their own local clientele to consider and please. The local depart-ment stores have their own view of what fashions are suitable for Fort Worth or Cleveland, and New York would be rash to assume that local taste does not matter. Local pride backs local talent, Marion Talley or Carole Lombard. And only when an issue has come home to the hearts and minds of local people, in a local voice, in terms in-telligible to Kokomo and Paducah, is it wise for an American govern-ment to act.

It is an old story, of course. Inland cities have been pioneers in many things. St. Louis was the first center of Hegelian studies in America—and even in the eighteenth century the little French fron-tier town was quite as much abreast of the intellectual times as was a French provincial town like Clermont-Ferrand. Chicago was, for a few years, the poetry capital of the United States, and Hollywood is a permanent rival of New York in all fads, fashions, and follies. New England cities like Hartford, Springfield, Worcester have not surrendered their autonomy of judgment to New York, much less to Boston. Civic pride and rivalry keep more places than Fort Worth and Dallas on their toes, often with admirable results. There is a story of a priest and a parson arriving in Dublin in a very crowded week and having to share a bedroom; the maid found them in the morning, each asleep on his knees beside his bed. American cities, in the same predicament of rivalry, are found awake, not asleep—though the rivalry may not produce uniformly good results at the same time. Thus, as far as I know, Cleveland and Cincinnati have never been in a state of municipal reform simultaneously; but each has had its reforming zeal given fresh edge by the contemplation of its sinful rival—which is the next best thing.

All people who have serious business to do in America, sellers and buyers of all things, cars and radio time, politicians and religionists, know that you must never forget that the American, more and more a city dweller, is convinced that he is a citizen of no mean city. And more and more he is right. He can remember, for example, what the Chicago lake front, now so splendid, was like before the Field Museum, the Planetarium, the Stadium were built on the slob-land between the Illinois Central tracks and the lake. He can remember what the Jersey marshes were like before the fantastic Pulaski Skyway, like an H. G. Wells vision swept over them. Smaller cities have similar sources of pride, like the highly unfunctional skyscrapers of a city like Beaumont, Texas, or the ship canal that links Houston to the Gulf of Mexico, or the Huey Long Bridge at Baton Rouge. Each city is, for its own region, a capital, a source of opinions and taste. Each city and each region is "from Missouri"—it has "got to be shown"; and until it has been shown, it is worse than useless, to go on the basis that all the best people in New York or Washington think that way already. The United States is not and will not be a vast Metroland. It is a nation of cities and of countrysides, spread over three million square miles, and so it must be hard to interpret and to unify, even in a great crisis. And even when it is really unified, each region will crab the deeds and the words of the others, especially of its nearest neighbors. The job of the leaders (and a most difficult job) is to hold together:

"this land,
My own Manhattan with spires, and the sparkling and hurrying
    tides and the ships,
The varied and ample land, the South and the North in the
    light, Ohio's shores and flashing Missouri,
And ever the far-spreading prairies cover'd with grass and corn."

To repeat, it is hard to do, and it has to be done by persuasion and not by coercion. But for a great cause, it can be done.

8

THE FRAMERS of the American Constitution put as their first aim the provision of the political means to "a more perfect union." They did not aim at perfect union, at the ironing-out of all regional differences, at the destruction of all regional independence. One of the organizers of the movement that led to framing the Constitution did, indeed, want complete union, did want to abolish local autonomy. But the ideas of Alexander Hamilton were so remote from any possibilities in the America of 1787 that they were more or less politely ignored by his colleagues, and Hamilton left the Convention in disgust. When the Constitution was put before the people, Hamilton was an effective fighter for it and as the first Secretary of the Treasury he helped to get the machine running. But he was not a maker of the Constitution because he thought it was not good enough, that what the United States needed was complete union, the fusion of the thirteen states into a unitary body politic.

Although Hamilton did not get his way, it was not necessarily a silly way. For the weak federal government that went into operation in 1789, like the strong federal government in operation in 1944, was a clumsy method of carrying on the business of the American people if all that is to be done is to carry on that business. It is clumsy to have the machinery of government in forty-nine units: the States, and the Union. It is clumsy to have the powers of the federal government loosely defined, so that they are constantly matters of controversy, so that many things are not done because it is uncertain what organ of government has the legal power to do them. It is at best inconvenient that the uncontested powers of the federal government are divided among a President, a Senate, and a House of Representatives, and that the question *what* power is *where* is decided by the majority of a Supreme Court of nine members. A government so organized must often be slow and uncertain in its action, indeed sometimes be incapable of action or, at any rate, incapable of action in time to meet the situation. The existence of an irreducible minimum of power in forty-eight states causes grave inconvenience, since it means that law and political practice vary from state to state. And some of those states are small in area, or in population, or in both; some are also the results of historical accidents; some break up the natural unity of geographical areas in a way to horrify a geopolitician or a political realist of the type that abolishes ancient European nations in an editorial. It is absurd that the empty mountain state of Nevada should be able both to make a good thing out of its lax divorce laws and to hold the United States to ransom to buy its other main asset, silver, at an exorbitant price. It is absurd that the three counties that make up Delaware should be empowered to charter corporations to do business all over the Union on terms more profitable to the corporation's controllers than to the body politic. It is absurd that the New York harbor area should be under the control of two states *and* the federal government, and that the pride of Arizona should hold up, for years at a time, the development of water-power that southern California badly needs.

But to cure these absurdities it would be necessary to impose on three million varied square miles a central authority strong enough to suppress local objections. But such a government would have a pretty free hand in deciding what local objections it decided to suppress—and such a government would be too strong for local liberties, so the American people decided in 1789 and have kept on deciding since.

The standard of comparison we should apply to the degree of success with which the American people have achieved "a more perfect union" is not that of a comparatively small, unitary country like Great Britain or New Zealand. We must look at countries with something like the same problems of space to deal with. We must look at Russia, at Canada, at Brazil, at Australia. And if we do look at them, we find that the Soviet Union with its central Russian mass and its control by the Communist party machine, and Brazil with its dictatorship—that both of these are, from the American point of view, buying union at the expense of liberty. On the other hand, Canada and Australia, while free, are not, by American standards, united; neither, for example, has dared to exercise in this war that last and most difficult power of government, the imposition of general conscription for service all over the world. Australia, at the moment, is in the throes of an attempted constitutional reform designed to give the federal government temporary powers adequate for the times. And Canada, despite the formal powers of its federal government, has had to allow Quebec to exercise a power of nullification which, in kind if not in extent, is like that claimed long ago for South Carolina by John C. Calhoun. South Africa, with a formally unitary government, is divided three ways by race conflicts, by bitter historical feuds, and by possibly insoluble economic and racial problems. Should the world demand for gold and political sermons fall off, the Union of South Africa might have to face, all over again, problems that optimists think were "solved" in 1909.

To have created a free government, over a continental area, without making a sacrifice of adequate efficiency or of liberty is the American achievement. It is a unique achievement in world history.

And because that achievement is tied up in fact and in legend with the Constitution, with the political system which makes the Constitution work, with a long historical experience (long, as modern political history goes), the American people are entitled to more than tolerance: they are entitled to sympathetic understanding in their worship of their own system of political and social institutions. And sympathetic understanding must begin with understanding of the obstacles to unity that faced and still face the People of the United States.

PART TWO

Unity and Liberty

*"May the Great Ruler of Nations . . . inspire
a returning veneration for that Union which,
if we may dare to penetrate His designs, He
has chosen as the only means of attaining the
high destinies to which we may reasonably
aspire."*

PROCLAMATION OF PRESIDENT
JACKSON TO THE PEOPLE
OF SOUTH CAROLINA, 1832

"WE THE PEOPLE of the United States, in order to form a more
perfect Union, establish Justice, insure domestic Tranquillity, provide for the common defence, promote the general Welfare, and
secure the Blessings of Liberty to ourselves and our Posterity, do
ordain and establish this Constitution for the United States of America." So runs the preamble to the American Constitution. When that
Constitution went into operation in the grand climacteric year of
1789, the "more perfect Union" aimed at was the political and economic unity of thirteen states, stretched in a thin ribbon from Nova
Scotia to Florida, bounded on all sides (on land) by the territories
of King George III of England and King Charles IV of old and new
Spain. The more perfect Union now covers the whole area from
Pacific to the Atlantic, three million square miles. The Spaniards
no longer hold St. Augustine or the British Detroit, and no one, or
practically no one, worries about threats to the territorial integrity of

the Union from its Canadian or Mexican neighbors. The forty-eight states, as well as such outlying dependencies as Alaska (so near to Siberia), Hawaii (too near to Japan), Puerto Rico, and Guam, and such linked political associates as the Commonwealth of the Philippines, have been welded together in a fashion that would have seemed miraculous to the Founding Fathers. No one now doubts the durability of the Union or its power to expel the Japanese from Manila or from Wake Island.

But there is a sense in which the "more perfect Union" has yet to be achieved, for the American people are not yet a unity, are not yet mingled in a true community of common purpose, common standards, mutual trust. In 1789, the population of the United States was overwhelmingly British in origin. French Huguenots had played a very important part in the political and intellectual life of the colonies, especially in South Carolina. German settlers had played a statistically more important part, especially in Pennsylvania and New Jersey. Dutch settlers had played a very important part in what was once New Netherland and is now New York. There were a good many Scots and still more "Scotch-Irish"—Ulster Presbyterians. There were a fair number of "mere Irish" like General Sullivan and Charles Carroll of Carrollton. And there were a good many Welsh. But, though the English strain was most dominant in New England, it was dominant everywhere.

In the nineteenth century, thirty million immigrants entered the United States and increasingly they came from parts of Europe that had contributed little to the population of the thirteen colonies. It is doubtful if the beneficiaries of the Constitution today, the present "People of the United States," are in a majority of cases the posterity of the American people of 1789 for whose descendants' liberty such thought was taken.

The three most important racial groups of recent immigrant origin are, at the moment, Germans, Italians, and Poles in that order. And although there were in America a few Italians like Jefferson's friend, Philip Mazzei, and although the Polish leaders Kosciusko and Pulaski played an important role in the American Revolution, there were, for all practical purposes, no Poles and no Italians in the United States of 1789. And although there were many Germans, natives like

Muhlenberg or newcomers like the Baron von Steuben, the Germans in 1789 were a small though not negligible minority. Anyone with a knowledge of the light that family names cast on Irish history can see that, in the very Protestant America of 1789, there were many Irish whose recent ancestry must have been Catholic. Nevertheless, the United States in 1789 was above all English and Protestant.

In the century and a half that has passed, a great work of assimilation has been accomplished. No names could be more thoroughly American than Dwight Eisenhower, Chester Nimitz, Franklin Delano Roosevelt. In a Midwestern town, a degree of unity is achieved that includes everybody, of no matter what racial origin. Or almost everybody. For the Catholics, the Jews, and the Negroes are still, to some extent, regarded as being outside the local community life, and so are the recent immigrants whose language, habits of life, and economic status remind the spectator that it is less than a generation since mass immigration stopped. So, too, are Southern poor Whites, pushing north into the new industrial towns where the "old-time religion" has to struggle hard and not always successfully to keep its place, where the colored population has (from a Southern point of view) forgotten its place, and where so many aspects of town life, from the High School curriculum to the standard diet, underline the difference between the rural "Anglo-Saxon," Protestant South and the new America in which all the peoples of Europe have contributed blood and habits of life and speech.

There is an apparent paradox in the contrast between the remarkable physical uniformity of American towns and their variations on the moral and psychological sides. Outside the South and the far West, the traveler getting off a train in the dark or driving into a town from the airport might well be in doubt as to what state, even what region, he was in. The towns look remarkably alike. The red fronts of the "Great Atlantic and Pacific Tea Company" are common to all. An expert in the distribution of the chain stores might guess something from the name above the "Five and Ten," for it is only in England that Woolworth's is always Woolworth's. The classical façade of the local banks, the neo-Gothic of the churches, the elegant brick and granite of the new post offices that Mr. Farley put up—all are lacking in local flavor. Is this Indiana, or Ohio, or York

State? One might get a clue to its being a southern town from the number of Negroes and from an indefinable air of something that it would be unkind to call slowness and, sometimes, too flattering to call leisure; or to its being in the West from the aridity of the land-scape and the semi-cowboy character of the male costume; or on the Pacific slope, from the geniality of the climate and the exuberance of the population. What is surprising, however, is not the amount of variation but the uniformity achieved over three million square miles.

The physical uniformity, true, conceals a good deal of racial variety. In New England, that block of church and school and con-vent is a citadel inside which the *Canadiens,* the "Canucks" of their "Anglo-Saxon" neighbors, barricade themselves against denationaliz-ing forces and preserve in Maine or Massachusetts the *ethos* and the language of Quebec. In Minnesota, Swedes keep alive some of the old ways they learned in Scandia, and in their Lutheran churches and denominational colleges resist complete cultural assimilation. Whole cities, like the Polish enclave of Hamtramck in the midst of Detroit, are ruled by one racial group and seem to the zealots of mere uniformity to be "un-American."

But more common is the town in which a dozen groups have to live together in close contact, in which a street of Germans borders on a street of Irish, in which the Italians and the Greeks are mingled in school and market, in which Jew and Gentile have to learn to get on together. It is in towns like these that the problem of Amer-icanization is most acute, in which the well-meaning efforts of Rotary Clubs and women's organizations fail in face of the facts that seem to suggest that, whatever the legal fiction may be, there *are* first-class and second-class and even third-class Americans, that there is a scale descending from the "old stocks" down to the Negroes.

They are all Americans; from the European point of view, in what they have in common—in speech, in appearance, in habits of speech and posture, in ways of life and views of life—they are all much alike. The American Pole is more like the American Finn than either is like a pure Pole or pure Finn. America denationalizes quickly. Does it nationalize?

At times, there is a temptation to say "No." Then American society seems like a pipe line; in it the different kinds of oil are all moving in the same direction, but they do not mix, except at the edges; they are all moving to produce a common American refined article—but the Bayonne in which this job of political and social cracking is to be done either does not yet exist or is not equipped to handle more than a tithe of the crude oil coming in from a dozen different sources.

Not all Americans are at home in America or are accepted as first-class citizens. For America has not, any more than other countries have, found a means of uniting all its people on the basis of freedom. Its political and social tradition, which has so successfully set out to make men and women proud and glad to be Americans in this world, has not dealt or attempted to deal with all of human hopes and fears.

Nor is this all. American unity has, in a sense, decreased as the original religious homogeneity of the thirteen states has been diluted by non-Protestant, non-Christian elements. America is now the capital of world Jewry, and anti-Semitism is one of the problems that perplex the wise American, Jew or Gentile, and tempt the demagogue, lay or clerical. In New York, the concentration of nearly two million Jews has made it possible to pretend to ignore, over the large areas where none but Jews live, that outside those areas there are present the elements of jealous hatred which are the standby of the anti-Semite. Whether Jew or Gentile is exclusively to blame is not a subject for inquiry here. "Restricted holiday camps" that exclude Jews are neither the cause nor the result of camps advertising "dietary rules strictly observed" that exclude Gentiles. There is anti-Semitism among the Negroes of Harlem, one "underprivileged" people set against another. And there is the old cleavage between the old, assimilated, modern-minded Jews and the mass of "Jews without money," often bringing from the ghettoes of Poland the qualities bred in ghettoes which are not socially valuable in the modern world. Whether American Gentile society is so rich in social talent, in artistic taste, and in intellectual power to be able to afford, in the long run, the snobbish exclusiveness of so many clubs and fashionable suburbs is open to question. What is not open to question is the danger to American social and political life inherent in the exploitation of anti-Semitism by crypto-fascist organizations, as well as by bigoted devotees of peace and international brotherhood. Colonel Lindbergh may have been only obeying a memory of his father's vehement intolerance when he hinted that the Jews had better behave themselves (in the father's case, it was the Catholics who were warned). But the priests and ministers and Senators and Congressmen who have, in the not very remote past, accepted, more or less willingly, the aid of rabid anti-Semites have a great responsibility before the American people and before the other minorities who will learn, if they do not know it already, that when American frontier intolerance gets its head, it does not require much rational justification. The Poles in Detroit who treated the Negroes of Sojourner Truth as the Germans in Poland treat Poles; the soldiers in Los Angeles who beat up the Mexican "zoot-suit" wearers; the woman who wanted the speaking of Spanish forbidden in Los Angeles; the Ku Klux Klan who came in to profit by the pathological situation largely created by Catholics in some Midwestern states; the Protestants who, for whatever innocent motives, are ready with facile charges against Catholics—all are enemies of American union. They are also friends of Hitler—and some of them know it.

There are patches of the United States where settlers of one origin have concentrated so thickly that they have been able to carry over into their new environment a good deal of the spirit and tradition of the old. The German Pietists of Pennsylvania, the German Catholics round St. Meinrad's Abbey in Indiana, the Dutch in parts of Michigan, the Scandinavians in Minnesota and North Dakota, and, most tenacious of all, the French-Canadians in so many New England towns and villages—these in greater or lesser degree have resisted the complete transformation of their lives by Americanism. But not all emigrants have any very kindly memory of the homeland. The Pennsylvania "Dutch" (i.e., Germans) have no living memory at all of Germany; many of the Dutch have no kindly memory of the Holland that persecuted their rigorist ancestors. Many of the Germans believe truly, and more believe falsely, that their ancestors were driven from Germany after 1848 because of their liberal or radical political views, intolerable in a country where reaction was triumphant. True, an affection for Germany could survive such an ordeal, as it did in the case of so eminent a German-American liberal as Carl Schurz, who forgave Bismarck's Germany much that he would have condemned in the contemporary United States. And one very distinguished American scholar has told me how his father, normally completely indifferent to the land of his birth, developed a good deal of German patriotism in the last war between 1914 and 1917 as he got more and more tired of hearing all Germans described as Huns.

The unifying role of the Christian tradition in America has been less important in this century because of the character of the religious conquest of the frontier. The religion that followed the pioneers was emotional, uncritical, unintellectual. The old New England Puritanism, with its insistence on learning, with its emphasis on the provision of a clergy that could use and a congregation that could accept an elaborate theology and epistemology, had no competitive chance on the frontier against the Methodists and Baptists. Petrus Ramus could not fight Peter Cartwright. So typical a New England experiment as the foundation of Illinois College failed, in a sense; it had to be transferred from the Congregationalists to a more emotional religious denomination. Indeed, the optimistic, humanistic culture of Emerson was more successfully exported to the frontier by missionaries like Emerson himself than was New England religion in the more technical sense.

The Anglicans and Presbyterians did a little better but not much; Bishop Chase and Kenyon College were very important forces in the civilizing of Ohio, but Bishop Chase was not Bishop Berkeley. Princeton was more of a religious power house for the South and West than Harvard and Yale were, but for too long Princeton College remained wedded to a sterile, old-line orthodoxy that was unattractive to the ebullient temper of the frontier and curiously high and dry compared with the atmosphere of its Scottish academic parents. President McCosh was not quite adapted to the age of the two Cairds in Glasgow, or even Principal Tulloch and Principal Rainey in St. Andrews and Edinburgh.

The old, humanistic culture of the South had died; it lacked the moral energy that the frontier situation called for. And when a Congressman objected to the purchase of Jefferson's library by Congress, on the ground that it contained too many books by Voltaire, he was expressing a popular opinion. Only the immense prestige of Jefferson could have secured protection for his ideas and, as it was, his new University of Virginia had to abandon its original plan of employing Thomas Cooper, that dangerous Deist.

Religion became a matter of conduct, of good deeds, of works with only a vague background of faith. It became highly functional, highly pragmatic; it became a guarantee of success, moral and material. The world of which Henry Ward Beecher on one side and Colonel Ingersoll on the other were such representative specimens was not quite the world of Harnack and Renan, Newman, Liddon, and Gore, Loisy, Denifle, and Denny. Theological schools turned from theology to a form of anthropology—a moralistic and optimistic form, but anthropology all the same. That "the proper study of mankind is man" was the evasion by which many American divines escaped the necessity for thought about God.

In the twentieth century, this policy suddenly ceased to be adequate. The fight over "fundamentalism," whether it took the form of the so-called "monkey trial" at Dayton, Tennessee, or the listing of "evolution" as one of the serious causes of stress between daughters and parents in Muncie, Indiana, or the fight in the Princeton Theological Seminary over the place of orthodox Calvinism in the last home town of Jonathan Edwards, was a fight over a very real problem. In the making of America, views about the relationship of God and Man had played a great part. If the God of the first settlers, and the God of the frontier who had converted so many tens of thousands in the straw pens of so many camp meetings, was no longer the God of the new universities, of the new technology, what was to replace Him? Could anything replace Him but "Democracy" made into an object of worship, or business, or success? Nobody knew; nobody knows, yet.

And this conflict hindered assimilation, because it weakened an old bond of understanding if not of union. Into this Protestant world millions of non-Protestants were pouring. There were, for example, the poor Jews. They were rapidly being torn away from the ways of life learned in eastern ghettoes but not provided with new ways of life by an American society itself perplexed and drifting. The earlier Portuguese and German Jewish immigration moved into a society which was far more confident of its aims and standards. As far as the Jewish immigrants were orthodox, they were moving into a society which shared with them a common literary inheritance. Americans whose parents called their children not merely by common biblical names like Abraham but by rare biblical names like the Arunah and Azariah of the founder of the Baltimore *Sun* knew something about the Jews, were capable of a certain sympathetic understanding of the synagogue which was not possible a generation or two later, when Jew and Gentile alike had forgotten the Old Testament and when Galushas and Isaacs had become Earls and Miltons.

Of more importance was the maintenance of a nearly complete barrier between the non-Catholic five-sixths of the American people and the Catholic sixth. For while the Jewish immigrants in the majority of cases left Jewish orthodoxy behind in a generation or two, a very large proportion of the Catholic immigrants kept to Catholic orthodoxy. There were, of course, cleavages in American Catholic families like those in Jewish families. The uprooting of the shady hero of *I Can Get It for You Wholesale* is a special Jewish case, of which Mr. Farrell's pursuit of a way of life for a Chicago Irish boy brought up as a Catholic, and Mr. Dreiser's pursuit of a way of life for an Indiana German brought up as a Catholic, are more attractive examples.

But from the political and social point of view, the Catholic problem is one of segregation, voluntary or involuntary. It is to be seen in its most striking form in New England, especially round Boston where the Irish population, now settled there for a century or more, still carries a chip on its shoulder and is often represented in public by too noisy spokesmen who would quickly be taught their place in Dublin. It is reflected in an attitude toward the culture of the modern world which startles any European observer and, in private, provokes hostile comment that recalls the atmosphere of a society in which anti-Semitism is beginning to be a real danger.

There is the memory on the one side of the hard life in the mills, of the poor bargaining position in which their illiteracy, their poverty and their inexperience of the industrial world left the first Irish immigrants. There is, on the other side, the memory of the excessive pugnacity, even when sober, of the newcomers, as well as of the social problems created in what had been a homogeneous society by the arrival of hundreds of thousands of people with a different economic and social background and a different religion. This last difference was and is more important than it suits either side to admit. There is a real conflict of traditions. The New Englanders saw themselves as pioneers of religious freedom and, though a few Quakers like Whittier might have their doubts and a few domestic critics like the Adams family might see the picture a little out of focus, in general this view of the past was accepted. But to the incoming Irish it was very different. The old Bostonians were the people who burned down the Charlestown convent, in part because of the stirring preaching of orthodox divines like Lyman Beecher. They were the people who welcomed the happy combination of religious propaganda and pornography known as *Maria Monk*. They were the heirs of the Puritan and Whig tradition in England. Cromwell was one of their heroes —whereas, for the Irish, Cromwell was the man of the Drogheda massacre and of the Hitleresque slogan "To Hell or Connaught." The Irish remembered the breach of the Treaty of Limerick, while the New Englanders remembered the Revocation of the Edict of Nantes which gave Boston the Revere family. The more enlightened and learned New Englanders were capable of sharing Voltaire's indignation over the execution of Calas, but the Irish were more likely to remember Oliver Plunkett, Archbishop of Armagh, judicially murdered by the party whose greatest ornaments were Isaac Newton and John Locke.

So admirable a man as John Jay Chapman acted more like a New Englander than a New Yorker when he tried to teach the Bible and influence the Irish slum children of the Bowery, forgetting that they saw the religious history of modern times (as far as they knew anything of it) from a viewpoint quite other than that which came naturally to a Huguenot. And if they shrank from his simple Bible teaching, it was because they believed that in the lifetime of their fathers and mothers the Catholic Irish had been subjected to the most formidable dragonnade of all, the ordeal of conversion by famine. They may have been wrong, but there is no evidence that John Jay Chapman ever tried to find out why he was so coldly received, any more than the publishers of *The Protestant* do today.

Even the German Catholics, who had had a much easier time than the Irish, had not been the recipients of much sympathy when Bismarck put their bishops and priests in jail with the approval of the Liberals of the time—except really acute ones like Walter Bagehot. And no Catholics noted much real enthusiasm among liberals for the cause of religious liberty in the states of Vera Cruz or Tabasco during the height of the Mexican revolution. Nor did the argument that the Mexican Catholics must have deserved this treatment impress them as conclusive, any more than the same argument pleased liberals in the mouths of defenders of Hitlerian persecution of the Jews—or Catholics.

The average American Catholic does not think of himself as being on the side of the Inquisition; he thinks of himself as being a victim of persecution. The tone of a paper like the Brooklyn *Tablet* strongly suggests that the inquisitorial temper is there all the same, but the Manhattan liberal press gives the Brooklyn *Tablet* more ammunition than its directors realize. It is, for example, a mistake to launch an attack on a priest suspected of fascist leanings, sign the attack with a markedly Jewish name, and forget to give the priest the customary title of "Father." It is also a mistake, if you want to win intelligent Catholics, to imply that they have much more control over and more responsibility for their co-religionists in Spain or Boston, than Union Seminary has for the antics of serpent-handling Protestant zealots in Tennessee.

Whatever the causes, the barrier is there. The Catholics' policy of supporting (entirely out of their own funds) schools of all grades and colleges and universities professing to be in competition with the great State and private universities has led to grave suspicion among the non-Catholics. Since all or practically all the teachers in Catholic schools are Catholics, while in New England, New York, and Chicago they constitute a great proportion of the teachers in the ordinary state undenominational schools as well, they seem to be, at considerable expense to themselves, both insulating their own children and influencing the children of others. In a New England town like Holyoke it may cause serious ill-feeling if it is suspected that appointment and promotion in the public schools is under Catholic control, since, as far as ecclesiastical authority prevails, there will be no Catholic children in those schools. Of course, this clerical ideal is never reached and the Protestant would-be teacher in New England is better off than the Catholic would-be teacher in rural Kansas or Georgia. She has a chance of getting a job, the Catholic has none. But since the Protestant tradition is native and the Catholic tradition exotic, the grievance is very differently felt.

Catholic suspicion, Catholic resentment, Catholic conviction that Catholics will not get fair play produce an indifference to influencing public opinion that is bad for the democratic process. The Catholic spokesmen appealing to their own people are victims to the American passion for oratory and vehement public polemics. There is not much in common between the controversial methods of Cardinal Newman and those of Monsignor Fulton Sheen, not to mention Father Brophy and Father Coughlin. The American public, the American politician, the American newspaper has to allow for Catholic opinion because there are so many Catholics, not because Catholic opinion has any interest as such. And Catholics do not explain nearly so often as they denounce and deplore.

Even if they did explain more, they might not do it very well, for the Catholic church in America is still, in the main, a church of poor people not interested in refinements of doctrine or apologetics. Thus when an American seminary professor was asked to contribute to a coöperative Catholic work of learning published in England, his contribution was so old-fashioned that it would have caused a mixture of amusement and distress in the Catholic faculties of his ancestral home in Germany. Not thus did the theologians and exegetes of Bonn or Freiburg or Munich write. The English editors had, in fact, to scrap the volume and get it rewritten. And it is permissible to wonder how many Irish-American bishops would appoint (if they could find one) so learned and critical a Hebrew scholar as Dr. Kissane to a chair in one of their seminaries. He is sound enough to be President of Maynooth, but is that enough for American Catholicism?

It is unfortunate, then, that the American Catholics are, by their training, so ready to suspect the worst of their neighbors and that their neighbors suspect the worst of them. On the one hand, the politicians, priests, and publicists see infidel, Moscow-fed hands clutching everywhere; on the other, more Americans than are quite conscious of it have fed on the mythology to which Mr. Upton Sinclair used to lend assent.

It is especially a strain in the field of foreign policy. For there a real conflict of policy, of prudence, of judgment of the realities may be made impossible by Catholic suspicion on one side, by Protestant suspicion on the other. A policy which, whatever its motives, may end in the destruction of the possibility of Catholic life in Poland, for instance, or the physical destruction of Rome, will be seen very differently by those who care for Catholicism and for Rome and by those who don't. The American Catholic, with a good deal of naïveté, tends to make the attitude of a foreign government toward the Catholic church a touchstone of its decency, as Jews do the treatment of Jews. When he is rebuked for this often very unrealistic attitude, when a Catholic institution like the great football college of Notre Dame gets rid of Professor MacMahon because of his critical views of General Franco, Protestant suspicion of American Catholics is increased. Not many Protestants in such a naturally scornful and suspicious frame of mind remember that Notre Dame is in Indiana, and that the five Sullivan brothers who went down in the *Juneau* came from the Middle West. Indiana, twenty-odd years ago, was governed by the Ku Klux Klan bent on saving America for the *Herrenvolk*, "white, Gentile protestants"—the only *real* American citizens.

2

IN ALL DEMOCRATIC COUNTRIES there is a fashionable readiness to sing "frustrate their politics, confound their knavish tricks." It is not to be taken too seriously, either as a judgment or as an expression of popular sentiment. Indeed, it is one of the attractions of a democratic society that it gives a place to the natural human emotion of critical resentment by the ruled of any pretension to infallibility in the rulers. A democratic society is one in which "the populace rise at once against the never-ending audacity of elected persons." And although the Longo case suggests that Walt Whitman might have been unwise to try anything of the kind in Frank Hague's Jersey City, in general the American, if he does no more than deflate his rulers by irony, does that.

But however pleasant and reviving this practice may be to the irritated if not oppressed citizen, it conceals from the superficial and cynical observer some important truths. Above all it conceals the truth that the United States was made by politicians. It was a comparatively small group of politicians who organized the popular rising against the authority of George III. And some of those political leaders, Sam Adams for instance, might not have been totally at a loss in Mr. Crump's Memphis, Mr. Hague's Jersey City, or Mr. Pendergast's Kansas City (before this last statesman had to go to the penitentiary). It was a group of politicians who created the demand for the new Constitution, who drafted it, who made it work. It was a group of politicians round one of their number, Alexander Hamilton, who provided the new Union with adequate financial resources and powerful vested interests; it was a group round another and more capable politician, Jefferson, who provided the necessary diplomatic and constitutional facilities for the rapid expansion of the American farmer to the West. It was politicians who postponed the outbreak of the Civil War, and it was one politician, at that time a rather obscure one, more or less accidentally elected to the office of President, who decided that the Southern states should not be allowed either to secede peacefully or to stay in the Union on their own exorbitant (as President Lincoln thought) terms.

Indeed, the role of the American politician and party is best exemplified by the history of the years leading up to the outbreak of the Civil War. It was not till the parties began to break down, till the Whigs disappeared and the Democrats were torn by schism, that civil war became practically certain. When in 1860 the Southern Democrats refused to accept Stephen Douglas as the party candidate, when the Douglas Democrats in the North refused to admit the right of the South to veto the will of the majority of the party, the case became really desperate. Churches, learned societies, clubs, these had split already. There was the atmosphere of Civil War in the Senate when Senator Sumner of Massachusetts first attacked Senator Butler of South Carolina with virulent rhetoric and was then nearly beaten to death by Representative Brooks. There was actual Civil War on a small scale in Kansas, where that eminent, zealous, and murderous land-speculator, John Brown, slew his enemies and, a year or two later, was captured by Colonel Robert E. Lee when he tried to instigate a servile war in Virginia. John Brown was an assassin to the South, a martyr to much of the North. But not till the Democratic politicians could no longer even pretend to coöperate, not till Lincoln, a politician of politicians, refused to accept compromise on the fundamental issues, was all hope gone. What the politicians could not do, no one could do; then it was a question of war, the final argument of kings and commonwealths. It was the political passions of the politicians, the political interests of the parties, North and South, that made the problem of reconstruction in the South after the Civil War almost insoluble.

It may be argued that before the Civil War the main direction of American policy was in the hands of the Supreme Court. In a sense it was; the Court alone had the continuous authority that was needed. But the Court succeeded as far as it was politically minded and wisely politically-minded. It had to remember what its greatest chief said: "We must never forget that it is a *constitution* we are expounding."

When the Supreme Court disregards the implications of this famous dictum of Chief Justice Marshall, and either takes refuge in a kind of high and dry constitutional pedantry (as it did between 1933 and 1937), or plays politics too openly and usurps the functions of other departments of government (as it did in the Dred Scott case in 1857), American reverence for the Court is badly strained and its utility diminished. And utility is the justification for the Court, as it is for Congress and the President; all must contribute to the unity and peace of the United States.

This overriding purpose justifies one aspect of politics that the pedantic purist often condemns, the catering to minority groups. In the Supreme Court itself, it is politically necessary that there should be at least one Catholic and one Jewish justice, that the South and the West should be represented, and that the Court should not be exclusively of one party. This is desirable because justice must seem to be done, not merely be done. It does not mean that the Court will divide on these lines. The present radical minority of the Court consists of one Catholic from Michigan, one former member of the Ku Klux Klan from Alabama, and one ex-Yale Law School professor from the state of Washington, all Democrats, joined, from time to time, by a former Republican Attorney-General from New York, now Chief Justice of the United States by appointment of President Roosevelt.

At a much lower level, the practical politician has to "seed" his list of candidates for all kinds of offices. In a polyglot city like Cleveland or Detroit, he must see that all important national groups are represented, possibly at a loss of formal efficiency, but at a gain in solidarity. To ignore the gain is to ignore simple facts of human nature that were not ignored at Versailles, except by mere academic critics. For a Pole or a Slovak to see one of his own kin as a judge or alderman or Congressman is to be ready to believe that American democracy has some meaning. For a Negro to know that there is one Negro Congressman, one Negro regular army general, is no doubt to be led to think that there are far too few, but how much better than there being none at all! For the grievance of exclusion from the jobs is a very real grievance, and to diminish the sense of grievance of minorities which are otherwise underprivileged is to promote the unity of the American peoples. The politicians have done this more consistently and better than any other class of Americans. The generous naturalization policy, and, in the old days, the privilege of voting without naturalization, made it profitable for the political managers to cultivate voters who, in other ways, were made to feel snubbed in America. As Charles Eliot Norton pointed out, the haughty attitude of the old New Englanders toward the Irish immigrants was bad for the political and social health of Massachusetts. But the politicians could not be so snooty as the Brahmins. Henry Adams might ignore the forces that were transforming New England into New Ireland, but his brother, John Quincy Adams II, the Democratic leader of the State, could not do so. Neither could the ambitious pupil and friend of Henry Adams, young Mr. Lodge.

For he needed, in emergencies, enough Irish votes to offset the influence of politicians like Patrick Collins. Senator Lodge might regret to see the Irish tide lapping round Nahant, but there were voters to be won over by judicious twisting of the British lion's tail.

Of course, there was another and less desirable result of this cultivation of minority groups. As Lodge himself pointed out in 1919, the existence of strong racial minorities in America made the adoption of any positive American foreign policy dangerous and difficult. And it is true that racial feeling plays some part in the views of the American people about the outside world. Negroes care about Abyssinia. The Irish dislike of England is not what it was, but it has not completely disappeared. American Poles are less likely to believe all that the intellectuals tell them about Russia than are American Czechs. And politicians know all this, have to allow for all this. It may make them despair of Europe, where there are no skilled manipulators to adjust the *amour propre* of competing racial groups. But although they may despair of doing anything with the warring nations of the old world, they at least do not believe that the day of nationalism is over. They know it is not over in Chicago, and they reasonably doubt whether it is over in Prague or Warsaw. But in the meantime they go on with their indispensable job of making minor concessions, often very formal concessions, sometimes corrupt concessions, but all helping to turn Polish-Americans and German-Americans into good Americans—and reliable voters.

So Congress and the State legislature have their quota of members who represent special interests. These politicians may not have any wide general views. They are far more likely, for instance, to share the feelings of the small and middling businessmen than those of the executives of the great corporations. The "Managerial Revolution" has not yet reached Congress, where the pleasing semifiction that the career of economic independence is open to all still has many believers. But all of them got to Congress by having something that the voters wanted, and what the voters wanted, while it is often not what Aristotle would have prescribed, is not to be neglected all the same. That the American people in some regions choose the spokesmen they do is regrettable, but it is a fact to be deplored, not ignored. One cannot even be certain that it is invariably to be deplored.

There is one region where racial and historical disunion is always a problem, is the cause of other problems, and is at moments the cause of a feeling of despair which, in face of any other American failure, would be premature and absurd. The South is analogous to the poor, feud-ridden, historically unfortunate border countries between Germany and Russia. It is poor, it is backward, its private troubles irritate the rest of an optimistic people. It has its own version of the common tongue; it is statistically inferior in a statistically-minded people; in the great national crisis that saved the Union, it was the enemy. But the main southern problem is the color problem. It is unhealthy for the South that over a third of its inhabitants are debarred, with more or less legality, from full legal rights. It is unhealthy for the South that law is too often defied by lynching, and that law is often more odious than lynching, adding hypocrisy to murder. It is unhealthy that the color question should force on the South a denial, in practice, of the American political religion of equality, pay such rewards to demagogues, and put such temptations in the way of honest men.

All intelligent Southerners, all Southerners whose sectional patriotism has any relationship to the problems of this age and is not purely archaic, know that unless the economic, educational, social, and moral level of the Southern Negro is rapidly raised, the South must continue poor and backward. But to assert this (as so many Southern whites have discovered) is to be dubbed a "nigger lover." And under abusive epithets of this kind and freely offered tributes to Southern womanhood, the real problems of the South are kept off the agenda of politics. When the South Carolina legislature goes on record in 1944 as being against "co-mingling of the races upon any basis of equality as un-American" and solemnly pledges its collective life to maintaining white supremacy, "whatever the cost," it undoubtedly speaks for most Southerners. But more modern-minded Southerners, in more modern States than South Carolina, would prefer not to fight on the issue presented by the resolution. For it does not do to announce that you will fight, "whatever the cost," on an issue like raising the average wage of Negro teachers from the present $70 a month to the white teacher's $90. It is after all an economy, not a cost, and perhaps the Palmetto State's very moderate standard of remuneration for its white teachers is in part a result of the determination to keep Negro teachers in their place.

It is a problem, too, affecting the whole nation, that the general "Anglo-Saxon" color prejudice, so great a political handicap in a world overwhelmingly "colored" and no longer in awe of the white man's murderous magic, should be reinforced by what is often an obviously pathological Southern version of it. And wartime tensions, the contrast between American promises and American performance, the justifiable Negro conviction that talk about race mixture and the like is a cover for economic exploitation, by American labor at least as much as by American capital—all make the situation more dangerous even than it was before. It is no wonder that so many good Americans, of both races, try to heal the breach, and take to heart Jefferson's ominous prophecy, his reflection on the national sin of slavery and on the justice of God. He trembled for his country; so do they.

The South, naturally and rightly, resents the view that it created the problem because of its own original sin. Not only was the sin national, but the manner in which slavery was abolished created a problem which, at best, was terribly difficult, almost insoluble. The slaves were freed by the military defeat of *all* the whites, not just a small class of masters. Emancipation did not merely ruin the plantation owners—it disorganized the Southern economy at a time when all Southerners, black and white alike, were impoverished by a long, wasteful and lost war. The victorious North behaved with far more economic ruthlessness than the victors of Versailles, and it imposed in the name of "Reconstruction" the rule of emancipated slaves, local renegades (the "Scalawags") and imported adventurers (the "Carpet-baggers"). Their governments were not necessarily much more corrupt than those which at the time afflicted some Northern cities and states but they were far beyond the means of the impoverished South. The North could get along with corrupt and wasteful governments that did nothing but plunder the treasury. But the South needed positive government, and it could not get it. Worst of all, the South did get that damnable gift, an alibi. It was given a reason for being permanently sorry for itself, like Ireland and Germany; it was given a permanent excuse for all internal weaknesses and faults; it was excused from assessing its own share in its troubles. Only today is the South slowly accepting the fact that the sins of "damn Yankees" and "uppity Niggers" are not enough to account for all Southern troubles.

The white South was not merely united by a common tragic experience. It had acquired from that experience a new order of values that it did not share with the rest of the United States. In the South, the heroes were nearly all soldiers. With the exception of Mr. Jefferson in Virginia, the southern pantheon was a soldiers' temple. No politician, not Patrick Henry nor Tom Watson, could compete for popular reverence with Lee and Jackson and even such politically ambiguous heroes as Longstreet. Even in Louisiana, the new fame of the martyred Huey Long has to fight with the old fame of Pierre Toutant Beauregard. And the people who filled the society sections of the papers, the Coca-Cola magnates of Atlanta, the steel magnates of Birmingham, were outshone in glamour by the heroic dead. Richmond might be the city of "Pin Money Pickles" for the believer in sky signs, but for its inhabitants it was and is the capital of the Lost Cause.

This priority was reflected in the high estimate put upon the career of arms. A nomination to West Point was a great honor indeed in the South. And of the eight colleges that prepare officers in an admitted rivalry with West Point, six are in the South. It was in one of them, the Virginia Military Institute, whose most famous teacher was Thomas Jonathan ("Stonewall") Jackson, that the present Chief of Staff of the American armies, General Marshall, was trained. And in this war, long before the mass of the American people saw how deeply its future was involved, the South was interventionist. It provided far more than a normal proportion of the American volunteers who joined the Canadian army and air force. The South knew that war *could* settle a lot; it had settled the South. It knew that it was not enough to say that one Yankee could lick three Japs or Germans, for had not one Southern Rebel licked three Yankees—and look at the final result! There was, too, a deep sense of kinship with the British people, and there was party fidelity to Mr. Roosevelt. Most Southern Democrats might not think much of the New Deal, but this was an old deal, the deal of war. So Dixie took her stand long before the rest of the Union. And the Texan was unjust to his own state when he said that if the United States went to war, he thought Texas would, too. It was the United States that joined a war that Texas had already entered, all but the formal declaration.

◇◇◇◇◇◇◇◇◇◇

3

THE POLITICIAN has to deal with "pressure blocs," and is often blamed for it. But it is only barely his fault that American politics is so largely a matter of pressure blocs, and—in addition—dealing with pressure blocs is a skilled job. It is a problem of political engineering, of estimating the pressure, the head of steam behind that drive, the kilowatt hours that such a project can rely on. It is not a mere question of taking a Gallup or a Fortune poll and discovering what a representative sample of voters will say if asked; the politician must guess what they will do, in the form of actual voting, in the form of support for lobbying, in the form of abstaining from supporting one party or individual and supporting another, in the form of casting the great, silent, and often decisive vote of the electors who stay at home on election day. He must estimate how hot the voters will feel in November about issues that appear to be burning them up in May. Two thirds of the Senators must guess how hot the voters will feel—whether indeed they will feel anything—in November two years or November four years ahead.

But it is not only that. It is a matter of estimating what real interests of the United States are involved. And this is the main preoccupation of the most important Senators. Nothing could be more absurd than to think that the chief spokesmen for the Isolationist point of view are stupid, or ignorant, or lacking in character. They include some of the ablest, best educated (in the academic sense), and most respected members of the Senate. If an average English Member of Parliament should undertake to debate with them, he would be displaying rashness not much less great than that of an average English heavyweight entering the ring against Joe Louis. These men may overestimate American strength and, more certainly, they overestimate the chances of a free American government working at all in a totalitarian world, but their mistake is not a naïve mistake. Indeed, in some cases it is the mistake of too acute, too legal, too learned a mind.

The role of all politicians, even when it is a mere matter of estimating the power of pressure blocs, has got harder in the last generation. In 1900, perhaps as late as 1912, the great traditional sectional divisions of the American people were still pretty much what they had been when the system broke down in 1860. There were the manufacturing states of the East. They had their own variations in sentiment and interest, but basically they wanted high tariffs and a strong central government. There was the South (then, even more than now, a region that was almost a nation). There was the Middle West, still, like the South, a producer and exporter of basic crops; there was the West, still mainly an exporter of minerals and cattle and wheat. But the new industrial revolution has made these simple lines of division no longer unalterable frontiers. Every state, or almost every state, has its important industrial interests, and those interests may lie as much in the export as in the import market. The agricultural interest is now (some hold) a burden on the total American economy, living off subsidies and tariffs without which it would be doomed to a serious contraction. And although hereditary voting—being a Democrat or a Republican because your grandfather was—is still one of the most potent forms of American ancestor worship, it is more and more common to find voters usefully classified by age and economic level, the young and the poor tending to be New Dealers if not perfectly orthodox Democrats.

The politician is now assailed by half a dozen competing interests within his own state or region; and his party affiliation, his own political philosophy, may give him no help in making up his mind as to what is going to be good for the public and even for himself. Some of the lack of party discipline that has been marked in Congress is due to this genuine confusion of mind. It has mainly worked to weaken the discipline of the Democratic party, but a Republican administration might find itself in much the same position, once the honeymoon period of party triumph was over. It is possible that the two historical American parties are going through a necessary period of disintegration and readjustment. It is an unfortunate coincidence that the whole world is going through such an adjustment, too, and cannot wait till the American party structure has been reconstructed before it undertakes to organize itself. Yet it may not be able to organize itself in any satisfactory fashion if the American internal conflict is not resolved some way, soon.

The separation of powers is laid down in the Constitution and is emotionally anchored in American political habits. But a development that is not constitutionally necessary and has no particular claim on popular support has made the separation of powers also a separation of personnel. The members of Congress (members of the House and members of the Senate alike) are more and more cut off from the Executive personnel. It is not only that with the decline of the "Spoils System" the administration of the federal government has more and more passed into the hands of permanent civil servants ("bureaucrats," as the politicians call them). But the political chiefs of the Administration are hardly ever chosen from the personnel of Congress. Only one President elected in this century (Harding) had ever served in Congress. Only one member of Mr. Roosevelt's cabinet has ever served in Congress (Mr. Hull). Only one of Mr. Roosevelt's chief presidential aides has ever served in Congress (Mr. Byrnes). Many Senators have held executive office in their own states or cities. A few have held cabinet posts in the federal government. But in the main there is a pretty complete cleavage between the personnel of Congress and the Executive. The case of the Republican nominees in 1940 was undoubtedly exceptional. But it is worth noting that the presidential nominee, Mr. Wendell Willkie, had never met the Republican nominee for Vice President, Senator McNary, before they were put on the same ticket. It is not surprising, then, that Congress (especially the Senate) should tend to be more critical than constructive, more legalistic than responsible in its attitude to current problems.

The Senate, as its name suggests, has a special place for old men or, at any rate, for elder statesmen who may, in fact, be fairly young though old in politics. It is supposed to and does take a long-term view. Elected for six years with a good chance (unless there is a party upheaval) of being re-elected, the average Senator may expect to be in office when the ordinary President has come and gone; and some of the senatorial irritation with Mr. Roosevelt may well arise from the unprecedented situation that he has been in the White House longer than most Senators have been in the Capitol. But there are Senators who date from the old days; some whose service goes back to the time of Wilson; at least one who can remember Taft, and, of course, quite a large number who can recollect the days of Republican Presidents. A veteran Senator may find it hard to accept the fact that much has changed since he entered the Senate, despite his own efforts to halt the change. Senator Smith of South Carolina was brought up in the shadow of the War Between the States and entered the Senate when Theodore Roosevelt was President, when there was an Emperor in China, a King in Portugal, when the Sultan reigned in a great part of what is now Yugoslavia, when Nicholas II was Tsar of All the Russias, King of Poland, and Grand Duke of Finland, when William II was German Emperor and King of Prussia, when there was a British Viceroy in Dublin, and when Lenin was working in the British Museum. Senator Hiram Johnson entered the Senate before the Russian Revolution of 1917 and reached the height of his powers when in 1920, as one of the heroes of the "Battalion of Death" who kept the United States out of the League of Nations, he was a serious contender for the Republican nomination which went to his colleague, Senator Harding. At that time Mr. Willkie was a young ex-soldier (and a Democrat) just admitted to the bar, and Mr. Dewey was still at school. These are exceptional cases, but the Senate does allow a good deal of play for the political veteran who gets elected over and over again—and it is easier to get elected over and over again from sparsely populated states than from populous states, and it is easier to get elected from states that never change their politics (like South Carolina, which is always Democratic) or from states like California where admiration for the state's Grand Old Man, Senator Johnson, is such that he is nominated by both parties. The Senate sometimes seems to the voter too tender of mere seniority, too tolerant of voices from the past. It would not matter if the Senate were a land of faery:

> *"Where nobody gets old and godly and grave,*
> *Where nobody gets old and crafty and wise,*
> *Where nobody gets old and bitter of tongue."*

But it is not. And the Senate may seem lacking in simple, optimistic faith to commentators who are too well provided with it. The Senate, however, exists to be sceptical. It has never died as a corporate body, never been dissolved, never lost continuity since 1789. It has seen many more than four-and-twenty leaders of revolt, and has seen a good many of them settle down to very unrevolutionary ways in the Senate. The Senate waits till it sees whether the American people is off on a real campaign, or on one of those short-distance crusades to which "Mr. Dooley" noted his countrymen's addiction.

It is this attitude of watchful waiting that earns the Senate such hostile criticism when it is applied to problems of international relations. For no treaty can be ratified without a vote of two-thirds of the Senate "present and voting"—which means, in practice, that thirty-three Senators, possibly from what are called the "acreage states," the more or less empty commonwealths of the West plus a few others, may hold up an international program approved by the overwhelming majority of the American people, advocated by the President of the time and eagerly awaited by that large part of the outside world which would follow an American lead if one were given. The long, exhausting, and apparently endless delays of the Senate's procedure in such cases do not merely exhaust the patience and energy of the American voter who may decide it is less laborious to let the whole project drop than to attempt to convert the irreducible minority of the Senate. It also has a natural if deplorable effect on the outside world, which comes, after a time, to the frame of mind of the man in the American hotel bedroom who heard another guest, in the room above, drop one shoe on the floor. He waited and waited and waited till his patience was exhausted, then called out, "Damn you, drop the *other* shoe!" At that stage the State Department has, regretfully, to inform the world that the United States has no other shoe because the Senate has refused to concur in the treaty negotiated with such anguish by the President and by the Heads of States less well provided with constitutional safeguards.

But, however the Senate minority may use or abuse its prerogative, it must be borne in mind that there is no effective substitute for a treaty binding the United States constitutionally and morally. Constitutionally, because no treaty has ever been invalidated by the Supreme Court and it is a doctrine of the Court that, within very wide and undefined limits, a treaty creates the necessary powers which it calls for. No "gentlemen's agreement," no "executive agreement," no "joint resolution" can do that. And still more important, no substitute for a treaty can bind the conscience and coerce the will of the American people.

There are drawbacks to this situation, but it has to be accepted that it is far more useful to get a limited treaty with the United States than the most promising, vague, and undefined substitute for a treaty. The treaty will certainly be more limited, more cautious, less inspiring. But it will be valid and lasting. Nothing else will be.

The problem of international organization is naturally seen by Americans in the light of their own experiment and experience. They know how political institutions grow in directions unforeseen by their makers. Few of the Founding Fathers would recognize today—and only one, Hamilton, probably would like—the federal government as it has grown to its present predominance. It was against such growth that the South fought the Civil War. Under the shadow of the Union, the states have shrunk in authority and prestige, and no amount of wishful oratory will ever give them back the sovereignty and prestige they owned yesterday. This process has been beneficial, inevitable (as that word is loosely used), irreversible. But it involved a great civil war testing the principle, as Lincoln put it when the war was drawing to a close, "whether any government not too strong for the liberties of its people can be strong enough to maintain its existence in great emergencies." The issue was already decided; the government of the United States *could* maintain its existence. But John C. Calhoun, had he lived to see that issue decided, would have asserted that the Civil War had proved that such a government would be too strong for the liberties of the states—a view which his successor in the United States Senate, "Cotton Ed" Smith, presumably shares.

Only if an American leader or leaders can persuade the American people—and the Senate—that the fears of John C. Calhoun, however justified, must be defied, that the caution which dares not do anything because there is a risk of its turning out badly, must be discarded, will the stability of the world, even for a generation, be underwritten by the United States. That hope for mankind is tied up with the problem of getting the American people, in its constitutional embodiment in the Senate, to accept the international implications of Thurber's law: "There is no safety in numbers or in anything else." But there are two orders of risk; the risk of certain disaster if nothing is done, and the risk of failure if something is attempted. This persuasion is a job for Americans. Above all, the job of converting the Senate is a job for Americans:

> *"Only those who brave its dangers*
> *Comprehend its mystery."*

The sophisticated Easterner, indeed the sophisticated American, when he looks at certain Senators and, still more, at certain Representatives, is likely to form a poor opinion of the discrimination of their electors. He supposes that the relationship between voter and politician is like that between the popular but silly preacher and his congregation as described by Charles II: "His nonsense suits their nonsense." There are cases in which this diagnosis fits the case, though it must not be forgotten that the voters may be perfectly well aware of the fact that their representative is not a totally serious character—but, then, is politics serious? One way to circumvent the wise man who considered making ballads more important than making laws is to get the laws and the ballads made by the same people. And good ballad-makers are harder to find than run-of-the-mill politicians. But it is also to be remembered that the sophisticated may be wrong, that the politician is not necessarily silly merely because he talks or dresses or thinks differently from the best people in the East, or even in the West. Mr. Bernard De Voto has pointed out how much Francis Parkman lost on the Oregon Trail by his Boston Brahminical superiority to the rough-and-ready frontiersman, who had not only bad manners but often bad morals, yet who deserved sympathetic study all the same.

The role of Congress is especially difficult in a time of great and rapid change like the present. For the role of Congress is to make laws and, then, after the event, to find out how they have been applied. As modern society gets more and more complex, the mere text of a law becomes less important. What Napoleon said of war: "A simple art, all is in the application of it," is almost as true of law-making. A generation ago, the great issues were legislative, issues whose administrative aspects were comparatively simple. Even as late as the Wilson administration, the great measures of the first great presidential term were legislative. Congress and the President worked together to pass measures like the Underwood tariff, the creation of the Federal Reserve System, the establishment of the eight-hour day on the railroads. But once the requisite statutory authority was given, the application of the new powers was fairly simple and comparatively uncontroversial.

But in the modern crisis, administration is nine-tenths of the law. This cannot be helped. Rigid definition of every possible case before the event merely paralyzes the Administration; it does not add to the authority or prestige of Congress. Indeed, by creating bottle-necks, it may diminish the prestige of Congress, for it is often forgotten, both on Capitol Hill and around the White House, that a loss of prestige by one branch of the government does not necessarily add to the prestige of another branch; it may simply lessen the hold of the whole political process on the imagination of the American people.

The Representative and still more the Senator is put on a spot. If he insists on hogging the limelight and opposing at length the legislative proposals of the Administration, he may be charged, often rightly, with holding up the measures necessary for the promotion of the general welfare. If he agrees to the Administration's proposals, he is accused of being a rubber stamp. If he investigates administrative mistakes or follies, he is accused of locking the stable door. If he replies to these criticisms by spontaneous action, by highly publicized vigilance, announcing the speedy end of the war or producing a recipe for victory with comfort, he gets a bad press. If he goes off on a witch hunt, he may create the effect of a government in which ballet-dancers are investigated by crooners. What is hard, almost impossible, to put across is the fact that most Congressmen and Senators have to work hard and seriously to keep their jobs, once elected, and that they get elected by giving an impression of being willing to work hard. The American elector, in good times, is not very critical of his representatives. His favor falls on the unjust and on the just alike. But all must be *and seem* "busier than a hound dog with fleas" if they want to please the customer—that is, the voter.

What they are busy about depends both on the Senator or Representative and on the voters of the state or district. In a state in which politics has, usually for historical reasons, been pretty free from ideological content (for example, Pennsylvania in the good old days), the Senators and Representatives were mainly busy with the serving of tables. But in more recent years it has been necessary to be busy with other things as well, to be a bit of a Mary as well as a Martha even in Pennsylvania. But although this is an improvement, it must not be forgotten that looking after local interests, local sentiments, local jobs, is a very legitimate concern of the American politician. Not merely will he not get re-elected if he neglects the local chores, but he should not be. One of the things that hold the vast area of the United States together is the belief that the political machinery provides a means whereby local and personal interests and sentiments are really taken into account in Washington. If all decisions of the federal government were handed down from some remote Sinai, the Government of the United States might rapidly acquire the appearance—and more than the appearance, the habits—of a remote imperial power; a power more "efficient" perhaps in that it would change its mind less often and make far fewer expensive mistakes. But it would all the time be making the basic mistake of not interesting the average man, three thousand miles away, in his government, if only by showing him that his government is human, fallible, and even feeble. The American may profess to admire efficiency at all costs, but one place where he wants his business suit let out at the seams is politics. If he did not want that, if he did not believe that these adjustments were part of the humanizing side of the democratic process, the American might quite quickly fall a victim to the German passion for leaving it all to the expert—which ends up in leaving it all to the inspiration of the Führer who tells the experts. After all, *somebody* has to tell them. In America, it is the politician. Of course, the politician may tell the expert too much, too often, and in tones that make it certain that experts will prefer to work for anybody rather than the United States. The wiser politicians know this; but not all politicians are wise, and one way of making the headlines is to put on a good show, vaudeville if higher forms of showmanship are beyond you.

Members of Congress are men (and women) of higher than average ability but, like men and women of all kinds with such ability in all countries, they are handicapped by the complexity of modern life, by the increasingly difficult character of its social problems, and by the absence of any generally accepted body of opinion, supported by all experts and intelligible to all reasonably industrious and capable amateurs. It is no wonder, then, that the American politician lends a ready ear to any Mephistopheles who whispers:

> *"Grau, theurer Freund, ist alle Theorie,*
> *Und grün des Lebens goldner Baum."*

So there is a ready welcome for slogans denouncing theorists who have neither (a) "had to meet a payroll," nor (b) "had to get elected to anything." There is something in each of these complaints, for in American society the place of the individual *entrepreneur* is still great in fact and even greater in fiction. And in a democratic society, having what it takes to get elected is a real quality, not to be assessed too lightly. Any given elected person may seem to be a proof that "you can fool all of the people some of the time" or "some of the people all of the time," but over any reasonably representative period, the American people get the Congress they want and (I hold) over the same period, better Congressmen than they deserve. There is another reason for the distrust of specialists that is humanly understandable though intellectually less defensible. Theory is not what it was a generation or two ago. When Cleveland defended his tariff policy by saying that it was "a condition not a theory that confronts us," Cleveland and his supporters and enemies knew a good deal both about the condition and about the theory. The theory was the theory of Free Trade vs. Protection. Nearly all the theorists (save for a few in

THE AMERICAN CHARACTER
By DENIS BROGAN

FOR several months I've had the enjoyment of participating once a week in a transAtlantic radio quiz between New York and London. People on each side ask each other questions about England and America. D. W. Brogan is one of the group who speak from London, and a high pleasure in the conversations has been the range and humor of his knowledge of the United States. That is not surprising, for he has studied and lived in this country, and he holds the important professorship of political science at Cambridge University. But how many teachers of politics and government are so familiar with the human habits and foibles that give history its color? Nothing in American life is alien to Brogan, whether technical points of congressional procedure, religious and racial prejudices, or our folkways in jokes, clothing, boasting, and food.

There is always a great deal in America that puzzles or alarms the cultivated visitor. The usual procedure is to express admiration while here, and be ironic about it later. This is not Brogan's method. He makes the most careful and sympathetic attempt to discern why North American habits and emotions are what they are. He finds that (as in every other land) they have grown out of actual conditions of living. In the course of his temperate and sympathetic chart of our metabolism he uncovers much which is valuable to all concerned. I don't think anyone has ever spoken more shrewdly, in such brief compass, of the still operative social effects of the long pioneer period; of the excesses of our climate; of our "Constitution worship," and of other forms of fetich, too, which he sketches without unmannerly emphasis. These, which are labor-saving conventions rather than genuine devotions, I myself would paraphrase as the worship of women, of repetitive phrases, and of continuous superficial information. Perhaps one should add the rather pathetic worship of youth; what other country always refers to its fighting men as "boys"?

The extraordinary, the portentous phenomenon we call the United States, alternately so maddeningly casual and so maddeningly rigid; fundamentally sentimental and good-humored; given to muddling through on a cosmic scale; with a passion for "parliamentary rules" but little true sense of parliament; gushed by well-known symbols or catchwords into frenzies of hyperthyroid patriotism — this gigantic spectacle is rarely examined with competent dispassion, least of all by ourselves.

Sometimes, just for me, I have imagined a little legend in which a shiftless and ignorant hillbilly, immersed (like all men) in his own hard concerns, was out in the Kentucky woods squirrel-hunting. In the blaze and hush of a November sunset he came to a hillside edge, saw through the tree trunks the great purpling spaces and cloud volutes of the West. For an instant, in a feeling almost sickness, he had some vague prescience of what that country might become. He thought, of course, that he must be coming down with the shakes; and hastily took a slug of corn whiskey. He hurried home through the slashes, piled knots on the fire, and told his wife he had a chill. Nine months later Abraham Lincoln was born.

Mr. Brogan, by admirable obser-

vations—"words that make us real to ourselves"—helps us look through the thick underbrush of present complications toward a wider notion of destiny. He knows that all national habits and instinctive responses grew out of hard necessity; they are likely to persist long after the need for them is gone. But they are still real, and it is not useful either to mock or to ignore them. Just as Mr. Churchill said that he had not been put in his post to preside over the liquidation of the British Empire, there are plenty of sincere voices here ready to assert that they do not intend to liquidate the United States Senate. But there will have to be a lot of liquidation of all sorts everywhere—in the sense of making some things fluid that had been too static. Mr. Brogan notes the pessimism of recent American literature — which he generously says is greatly the senior partner in the present English-writing world. It was due to the indignant discovery, by those who had leisure to discover it, that life is still tough. The Great Rock Candy Mountain was more rock than candy.

The severe problem — every nation's problem in days now upon us —is how to reconcile each people's hard-earned and legitimate nationalism with the requirements of a still greater world-society. Some of our various autonomies we must plainly surrender; there are also our own characters and identities that we must keep. "The critical period in the life of a national society," Mr. Brogan wisely says, "comes when it has to learn new habits, acquire new emotional attitudes. Such necessary change is painful for an individual and for a people." But he thinks we're big enough for the pain. Brilliantly he says of the United States, "melodramatic pessimism is often on the surface, but below it is the permanent optimism of a people that has licked a more formidable enemy than Germany or Japan, primitive North America." Our national motto, subconsciously, has always been "Root, hog, or die."

I believe this book will take its place among the enduring essays in national psychology. It is the sort of thing that only an outsider can do for any country; it seems to be done best of all, for us anyhow, by Scots with a touch of Irish or French. Burke did it; Bryce did it; R. L. Stevenson could have done it. What makes this lucid profile of the American temper a real job of catalytic cracking is its humor, both ironic and demure. Brogan has listened to all the customary noises heeded by philosophers, but also like Lady Macbeth he has heard the owl scream and the crickets cry. Think of it, a social historian who knows

that our precious boloniana are also of political importance. Who knows the difference between coca-cola and pepsi-cola, or Dodgers and Giants; how to pronounce Houston (Texas) and Cairo (Illinois); what they licked at French Lick, and who Pontiac was. He knows that sometimes writers such as Mencken, Thurber, Ogden Nash, Dorothy Parker, Vachel Lindsay, William Saroyan, or cartoonists Hokinson and Arno, are more important in the seminar of Americana than a dozen shelf-stayed historians. In his continuing study of the American mythos I would commend him to three shrewd commentators he seems to have missed: Strunsky, McFee, and the late Don Marquis.

This is the first genuine attempt since Bryce to understand the more intimate how-come of American emotions and behaviors. Occasionally one would enjoy arguing with Mr. Brogan on some point, but he could probably justify it. I adopt for him the immortal saying of Agatha Christie's great detective, Hercule Poirot: I should not like him to be wrong. It is not his *métier*.

CHRISTOPHER MORLEY

In accordance with a suggestion made by a number of our subscribers this monthly reprint from the Book-of-the-Month Club *News* is printed in this format so that it can be pasted, if desired, to the flyleaf of the book.

the Wharton School of Finance at the University of Pennsylvania) were Free Traders. The majority of the American people and American politicians were more or less opposed to the theorists. But there was no great mystery about the Free Trade case and only the necessary amount of mystery-mongering about the Protectionist case. And when John Sherman of Ohio insisted, year after year, that "the way to resume is to resume," the case for going back to the international gold standard was fairly clear. So was the question of what sections of the American people would gain (like Sherman's friends) and what sections would lose or thought they would lose, like the supporters of "Silver Dick" Bland who were to find their prophet in William Jennings Bryan.

But a discussion of tariff or currency questions today is like a discussion of relativity to an old-fashioned physicist or logician: it involves a recasting of the "normal" intellectual order, of the "normal" standard of rationality, of which few people, Congressmen or bankers, are capable. The average citizen, in or out of Congress, is puzzled. Those persons who claim to be experts do not all speak with one voice and, confronted with Keynes plans and White plans, with Professor Hansen and Professor Schumpeter, the politician is tempted to despair. And he is still more tempted to conceal his despair, to assume the role of the plain, blunt man, to cry "A plague o' both your houses!" and try something practical—which often turns out to be totally impracticable.

Here, again, Congress suffers from its lack of administrative authority. It has few or no experts of its own. It may hire some from time to time, but it has no permanent substitute for the hired experts of the Administration. Nor, even if it had, would its academic studies have the same weight as the reports and decisions of the law-enforcing bodies, of the agents of the Executive departments. As Professor Bliss Perry has pointed out, there is nothing unnatural or discreditable in this human reaction. And if there is any blame on one side or the other, at least as much attaches to the experts, who cannot get their points across, as to the Congressmen who seem slow on the uptake. As many of the experts were at one time college teachers, they cannot say that they have no experience in making things plain to non-specialists. After all, they have presumably to do some educational work with their own political chiefs as their English opposite numbers have to do all the time.

But be the causes what they may, the result is unfortunate. It leads to an American version of the great French political heresy that complex social and economic problems can be solved by rhetoric. It is not a case of silly denunciation of rhetoric as a spur to action, as a creator of democratic will, as a builder or sustainer of morale. It is unnecessary to stress the importance of this role in the age of Roosevelt, Churchill, Hitler, Goebbels, de Gaulle, Chiang Kai-shek,* and the numerous orators of the Moscow radio. But the place of rhetoric, though great, is limited, and this is too often forgotten. It is, for instance, often mere rhetoric to denounce a measure, which you dislike anyway and because you dislike it anyway, as "un-American," or, what is an intensive of the same adjective, "unconstitutional."

The worship of the Constitution by the American people and by the American politician is so natural and so valuable, so indispensable an element in national cohesion, that immense tolerance even of the abuse of that worship is necessary. And some politicians who fall back on the Constitution as an answer to all problems, and as a barrier to all change, are perfectly sincere. More or less consciously they are taking the advice that Chesterton gave to a now forgotten English politician:

"Walter, be wise, avoid the wild and new,
The constitution is the game for you."

But it can become a monotonous game, and a time-wasting game for the spectator who may wonder how the American nation ever got going and kept going if the job of finding authority for action was as arduous in the early days as it is made to seem today. Of course it was even more arduous, but the ways in which Hamilton, Jefferson, Jackson, Lincoln, Cleveland, Theodore Roosevelt, and Wilson managed to find authority for doing what they wanted to do, and what they believed the nation wanted or needed to have done, are now sanc-

* I have, of course, no views myself on the oratorical powers of the Generalissimo, but a colleague tells me that his radio speeches in Chinese are admirable, superior to his wife's speeches in English.

tioned by time and tradition and by the vested interest of great parties.

The division of responsibility between Congress and the President has an important influence on the way in which public opinion is educated, distorted, expressed. Since a congressional speaker normally will not have the responsibility for putting his warmly declaimed principles into action, he can be as hot, dogmatic, and unyielding as he pleases. Since debate is rare in the House of Representatives, since nearly all real business is done in the committees, it is natural that such debate as there is should be very oratorical, should be "sounding off," not discussion. And this is one of the reasons why public speaking in America is still so rhetorical, why audiences for example do not often "heckle" a speaker, bombard him with questions, or embarrass him with ironical applause or laughter. It is almost as rare to interrupt a political speech as it is to interrupt a sermon.

In the Senate, things are different. Any Senator who can get the floor can talk as long as his wind lasts. He cannot be out of order unless he takes the most extravagant liberties. So Senate debates are often lively, often educational. They are very different from the formal pieces declaimed in the other House, or even printed and sent to the voters without being spoken at all. A Senator has to persuade his colleagues, even those of his own party, or he has to intimidate them, and so the Senate has a high representation of public speakers who can discuss as well as declaim. Yet the national tradition is now for declamation. In the old days, joint debates like those between Lincoln and Douglas educated the public and kept the debaters in training. But those old days are past.

The result is that all issues are discussed with oratorical trimmings, reports to the nation are made in tones loud enough to have a chance of being heard over the competing din. Issues are necessarily simplified to fit these conditions; the speaker must know or appear to know all the answers, and he must set them down in a simple oratorical black-and-white. This is especially true if he is a candidate for the presidential nomination (and many are). For he will, if successful, be running for an office in which he will be responsible for all aspects of national policy. He cannot say or imply that his future colleagues will look after this department or that, for he won't have any colleagues, only subordinates.

It is inevitable, therefore, that difficult and complicated issues should be reduced, in public, to very simple moral issues, with words like "liberty," "constitutional," "states' rights," "the spirit of '76," "the American way," "malefactors of great wealth," "Bolsheviki," "the American home" or "women" or "children" doing duty for argument.

Yet all this is not to be taken too seriously. It does not deceive either the public or the orators. I can remember seeing and talking to a politician then much in the public eye (and still in it though less prominently) after a speech in which he had washed away a number of complicated questions in a flood of adjectives. And the orator, so confident, so simple-minded on the stump, was tired, disillusioned, puzzled, anxious. He had been playing the part assigned to him, but he was much more Hamlet than the simple-minded, quick-acting Othello for which he had been cast by his managers.

But oratory, phrases, the evocative power of verbal symbols must not be despised, for these are and have been one of the chief means of uniting the United States and keeping it united.

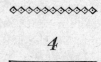

4

AMERICA IS PROMISES but America is words, too. It is built like a church on a rock of dogmatic affirmations. "We hold these truths to be self-evident, that all men are created equal, that they are endowed by their Creator with certain unalienable Rights, that among these are Life, Liberty and the pursuit of Happiness." "We the People of the United States, in order to form a more perfect Union, establish Justice, insure domestic Tranquillity, provide for the common defence, promote the general Welfare, and secure the Blessings of Liberty to ourselves and our Posterity, do ordain and establish this Constitution." These are only two of the most famous assertions of faith in things unseen, of dogmatic articles denied in good faith by many non-Americans but asserted in good faith by millions of Jefferson's countrymen from July 4th, 1776 to this day. How absurd an ambition for a people to attempt, by a written constitution, to "establish justice"! It is an ambition to make lawyers laugh and philosophers weep. "To promote the general welfare"; what is this entity so confidently labeled? What would a Marxian or a Machiavellian make of it? What an overleaping ambition of the Supreme Court to apply not known statute or case law but "the rule of reason"! What complacent courage in the founders of the Massachusetts Bay Company to identify the decision of John Winthrop, Richard Saltonstall, and the rest to transplant themselves to New England with "the greatness of the work in regard of the consequence, God's glory and the churches good"! Nevertheless, Massachusetts was founded, and a Saltonstall is governor in this year of grace, 1944, more than three hundred years later. There have been other consequences, too. What (possibly nonspontaneous) wisdom was shown by Lord Baltimore and the other Catholics of Maryland who in 1649 noted the evils arising from "the inforcing of the conscience in matters of Religion" and so came out for the toleration of all Christians—this in an age when the Inquisition was still going strong, a year after the Peace of Westphalia, the year of the massacre at Drogheda by Cromwell, a generation before the revocation of the Edict of Nantes? With what Hebraic confidence in their mission did the people of Massachusetts in 1780 acknowledge "with grateful hearts the goodness of the great Legislator of the universe, in affording us, in the course of His Providence, an opportunity, deliberately and peaceably, without fraud, violence or surprise, of entering into an original, explicit, and solemn compact with each other; and of forming a new constitution of civil government, for ourselves and posterity; and devoutly imploring His direction in so interesting a design, do agree upon, ordain and establish, the following Declaration of Rights and Frame of Government, as the Constitution of the Commonwealth of Massachusetts." Only a lively conviction of divine interest and direction could have justified so extravagant a hope as that by the mere separation of the legislative, executive, and judicial powers the people of Massachusetts or any people could establish a "government of laws and not of men."

But these aspirations, these hopes, extravagant or meaningless as they may seem to the critical, have been fighting words, hopes and beliefs leading to action. So have been the phrases, the slogans, authentic, apocryphal, half-authentic, with which American history and American memory is filled. This is no country where "what Mr. Gladstone said in 1884" is a comic mystery. These echoes from a heroic if overdramatized past resound still. "Give me liberty or give me death!" "In the name of the Great Jehovah and the Continental Congress!" "First in war, first in peace, first in the hearts of his countrymen." "Don't give up the ship." "We have met the enemy and they are ours." "Our federal union, it must be preserved." "Look at Jackson's men, standing like a stone wall!" "With malice toward none." "Public office is a public trust." "You may fire when ready, Gridley." "Don't cheer, boys! the poor devils are dying." "Make the world safe for democracy." "One third of a nation." The American man-in-the-street may not attribute all these slogans correctly. He may think it was Lawrence of U.S.S. *Chesapeake* who said "Don't give up the ship"; almost uniformly he thinks that it was Washington who warned against "entangling alliances," whereas it was Jefferson. And he *will* mix them up with texts from Scripture. He may have no more knowledge of the historical context than had the badly frightened citizen who, rescued from a lynching bee, protested: "I didn't say I was against the Monroe Doctrine; I love the Monroe Doctrine, I would die for the Monroe Doctrine. I merely said I didn't know what it was." Not all his slogans are reverent. He may, at times, fall back on "Oh, yeah" or the more adequate "however you slice it, it's still baloney." But he knows too much to despise the power of speech, to think that Bryan was adequately described when he was compared to the Platte River of his native Nebraska: "Five inches deep and five miles wide at the mouth." The power of even bad oratory is still great. The power of good oratory is greater.

So the American suspends his irony when a recognized public figure is speaking, or even when he is merely "sounding off." The American audience listens patiently, even happily, to dogmatic and warm statements in favor of the American constitution, home, woman, business, farmer. An American college president (from the deep South) has been known to impose a severe strain on the discipline of the undergraduates of an Oxford college by addressing them as "clean-limbed, clear-eyed boys." A pastor has been known to describe casting a ballot as a "political sacrament." Senator Vest's panegyric on the dog is only recently condemned as too lush, and a tribute to Southern womanhood is engraved on the pedestal of a statue to a forgotten statesman in Nashville, Tennessee.

In Chambers of Commerce, at Rotary Club meetings, at college commencements, in legislatures, in Congress, speech is treated seriously, according to the skill and taste of the user. There is no fear of boss words or of eloquence, no fear of clichés, no fear of bathos. In short, Americans are like all political peoples except the British. It is the countrymen of Burke and Gladstone and Asquith and Churchill who are the exception. But the difference has now the importance of an acquired characteristic. The British listener, above all the English listener, is surprised and embarrassed by being asked to applaud statements whose truth he has no reason to doubt, but whose expression seems to him remarkably abstract and adorned with flowers of old-fashioned rhetoric. It is in Congress, not in the House of Commons, that a speaker can safely conclude a speech on the reorganization of the civil service with a parallel between the Crucifixion and what the then incumbent of the White House had to go through. It is in all kinds of American public meetings that speakers can "slate" and "rap" and "score" and "blast"—to the advantage of headline writers. No words, it seems, can be strong enough to express the passionate feelings involved. It is not quite so bad or good as that; American politicians, American orators, are not so burned-up as they seem. But it must not be forgotten that they are often quite annoyed, quite worried, quite angry; that they are taking really quite a dim view, even when all they can find to express their mood, verbally, is a statement that the American way of life is due to end on the first Tuesday after the first Monday in November every four years. If an American—even a Senator—asks, "Is civilization a failure, or is the Caucasian played out?", it is not necessary to despair. All Americans dislike being beaten at poker and, for the greater gaiety of nations, don't mind saying so.

It is not merely that Americans like slogans, like words. They like absolutes in ethics. They believe that good is good, even if they quarrel over what, in the circumstances, *is* good. It was an American, true, who said: "My country, right or wrong. May she always be right. But, right or wrong, my country!" *

But this sentiment is in advance of that of many simple patriots in other lands who cannot conceive that their country could be wrong, who feel no possible risk of moral strain, and who would agree with the British naval officer who thought that even posing the question was improper conduct in an instructor of British naval cadets. To condemn a thing simply as un-American is often foolish, but no more foolish than to condemn a thing merely as un-English. And since the Americans are very articulate about the content of Americanism, while being English is a thing in itself, there is slightly more chance of there being meaning in "un-American" than in "un-English."

This national fondness for oratory, for slogans, has another cause or another result. It was an English Puritan leader on trial for his life who said of the execution of Charles I: "This thing was not done in a corner." It was a very American attitude. What Wilson preached—"open covenants openly arrived at"—is what the American people wants and expects to get. Like Wilson, it exaggerates the degree to which this standard of public negotiation is practicable. It is not always possible to negotiate under the klieg lights of congressional or press publicity. There are sometimes good reasons not only for secret negotiations but for confidential commitments. But they have to be very good reasons, advanced by leaders, native or foreign, in whom the American people have trust—and that trust will not be unlimited. No American leader, certainly not Washington or Lincoln, not Jackson or Jefferson at the height of their power, was thought to be above criticism or even above a certain degree of legitimate suspicion. Whitman, when he wrote of "the never-ending audacity of elected persons," voiced a general American belief that all leaders bear watching and that they are in duty bound to make frequent reports on the state of the Union, with or without aid of a fireside. The Americans are all, in this connection, from Missouri; they have got to be shown. They have also got to be told, and so has the world. Again, it is a powerful American tradition at work. Every

* I have used the popular, not the correct, version of the dictum of Commodore Decatur, U.S.N.

American child used to learn by heart and many still learn by heart a famous plea for telling the world. For the most sacred of all American political scriptures, the Declaration of Independence, opens with a preamble justifying publicity. "When, in the course of human events, it becomes necessary for one people to dissolve the political bands which have connected them with another, and to assume among the Powers of the earth, the separate and equal station to which the Laws of Nature and of Nature's God entitle them, a decent respect to the opinions of mankind requires that they should declare the causes which impel them to the separation."

The Americans expect from their own leaders—and from the leaders of other countries—a regard for the "Laws of Nature and of Nature's God"; they also expect a "decent respect to the opinions of mankind"—publicly manifested in reasons given and discussed with what may seem excessive freedom and candor of comment. It is a view which gives rise to awkwardness and annoyance, but that can't be helped. The ablest modern publicist, native or foreign, is no match for one of the two greatest writers of political prose who have been Presidents of the United States. And, since I have talked so much of the American passion for oratory, for the spoken word, it is worth recalling that Thomas Jefferson, one of the finest figures in American history, was also easily the worst public speaker of his time, perhaps of any time.

"A decent respect to the opinions of mankind." It is still a phrase to be remembered. It means that the American man-in-the-street expects to get the low-down on all secret conferences, to have international decisions supplied to him before the participants have had time to put their smiles on and pose for the group photograph. If this demand is not forthcoming from official sources, it is provided from unofficial sources. Commentators of varying degrees of knowledge, candor, truthfulness, ingenuity, intelligence, explain and announce. Wildly conflicting guesses are made with equal confidence, and the reader and listener is given a wide range of confidential misinformation—as is his right. The outsider may wonder at the willing suspension of disbelief on which the commentators can count. He may think that Tom Sawyer was a notably representative American in his insistence on romantic possibilities in face of drab and dreary realities.

He may wonder whether an eminent law professor has any particular authority for his views on the connection between British policy and Rumanian oil. He may wonder whether anybody wanting to keep a secret would tell it to Walter Winchell or even dare to enter the Stork Club. But these doubts are irrelevant. For the dispensers of secrets are catering to a public that has a village horror of the successful privacy of its neighbors. This public cannot see why Mr. Roosevelt should want to keep his political intentions quiet, any more than Mr. Tommy Manville keeps his matrimonial intentions quiet. Of course, he may *try*, as a football coach keeps his secret plays quiet if the scouts from other colleges let him. But it is the duty of columnists and Senators to tell all, as soon as they have discovered it or even before. And no agreement that needs to be kept dark for any length of time has any chance of success in the United States. For the American Republic is much more like the Athenian than like Venetian Republic. And Americans, though they have a great deal to do, have in common with Saint Paul's Athenian audience a continuous eagerness "to tell or to hear some new thing."

But there is more behind it than this passion for information, for an elaborate version of corner-grocery gossip. The American Republic was founded in the days of the "secret du roi," in the days when Wilkes was, with some difficulty, made a martyr of for revealing the secret of Parliament. A world in which great decisions were made by kings or oligarchies in secret, and the results communicated to docile subjects, this was the world against which the founders of the American Republic revolted. True, great things have been done in secret even in America. The Constitution was made in secret—it could not have been made in public even if the art of eavesdropping had in those days been practiced as expertly as it is now. But it was presented, quickly and in its final form, to the American people, presented to be accepted, or rejected or amended. Only so could "We the People of the United States" be committed. Only so can they be committed today.

❖❖❖❖❖❖❖❖❖❖

5
___

THE WORD "SCHOOL" in America covers every type of educational institution. Being "at school" may mean being at a kindergarten or at Harvard. School, too, has kept much of its Greek meaning. It is a system of organization and training for leisure as well as work. And it has become more and more adjusted to its environment, undertaking to do more than it can (which is very American) and doing much more than it seems to do (which is also very American).

The social and political role of American education cannot be understood if it is thought of as being primarily a means of formal instruction. If it is so thought of, it will be overrated and underrated. It will be overrated because the figures of two million college students, of seven million high school students, will dazzle the visitor used to seeing opportunities for higher education doled out (except in Soviet Russia) on a combined class-and-intellectual basis. It will be underrated if, at any stage below the highest (that is, below the great universities), the academic standards are compared with those of a good English, French, or pre-Hitler German school. If these millions of boys and girls are to be judged by their academic accomplishments, they will be judged harshly. But they are not to be so judged, for their schools are doing far more than instruct them: they are letting them instruct each other in how to live in America.

Of those millions, a large section will be the children of immigrants to whom English is still largely a foreign tongue. Of these millions, a very large proportion will be the children of migrants from different parts of the United States. Others will be the children of rural-bred parents, forced to adjust themselves to the new urban world. They have to learn a common language, common habits, common tolerances, a common political and national faith. And they do. It is this aim and this success that justifies the lavish buildings of the local high school; not merely the classrooms and the laboratories, but the gymnasium, the field-house where basketball can be played in comfort in the depth of the bitter winter, the swimming pools in which the summer heat can be endured.

It is true that the teachers are relatively badly paid and have an inferior social as well as economic standing, insecure tenure and politics making their condition worse. More money spent on men might get better results than more money spent on buildings. But it is easier to get the materials for buildings than the materials for teachers. As long as American society remains individualistic, competitive, confident that the answers to the present are in the future, not in the past, it is going to take more than money to seduce the right men and women in adequate numbers away from the life of action. And, a point too seldom remembered, the necessity for providing teachers for the two million college students hampers recruiting for high schools. In many cases, the colleges are doing what is really high school work and it matters comparatively little where the good teachers are, as long as they are teaching.

The political function of the schools is to teach Americanism, meaning not merely political and patriotic dogma, but the habits necessary to American life. This justifies the most extravagant items in the curriculum. Since the ability to play bridge is one of the marks of Americanism in a suburb, it is reasonable that there should be bridge clubs in schools. The main political achievement of the high schools and grammar schools is to bring together the young of all classes and all origins, to provide, artificially, the common background that in an old, rural society is provided by tradition, by the necessary collaboration of village life. The elementary schools—the "grade" schools—do this, too, but as far as an American town is broken up into racial blocs, the Ethan Allen Public School may have mainly Polish pupils, the Zachary Chandler mainly Welsh. Only in the Warren G. Harding High School is a big enough common pool formed in which Americans can be made.

Some of that Americanization is, of course, done deliberately and formally. Mr. Carlton Hayes pointed out long ago that the ritual of flag worship and oath-taking in an American school is a religious observance. Little boys and girls, in a school from which religion in the old sense is barred, solemnly rising each morning and reciting together the "American's Creed" * are performing a religious exercise as truly as if they began the day with "I believe in God the Father Almighty" or asserted that "There is no God but God."

And that these daily rituals are religious has been at last affirmed by the Supreme Court in a series of cases in which the children of a fanatical sect, Jehovah's Witnesses, had been excluded from schools for refusing to give to the flag honors that, so their parents had taught them, were due to God alone. In 1940, all the Court except Chief Justice Stone held that flag worship was among the things that were Caesar's. Since that year, however, they have decided by a majority that the religious rights of the children were being infringed. What is significant in the cases is not the Court's reversal of itself but the reality of the issue presented to it. For to the Court, and to the overwhelming majority of the American people, the objections of the Witnesses were as unintelligible as the objections of the Christians to making a formal sacrifice to the Divine Emperor were to Trajan and Pliny. The school board of Minersville, Pennsylvania, was faced with a real problem when it was asked to admit that children refusing to take part in the most sacred rite of the day should be allowed to associate with the believing children of the formally unestablished national church of the United States. So, too, was the state of Oregon when it found Catholic and Lutheran children refusing to go to the schools it provided. But in both cases the Supreme Court held, finally, that compulsory Americanism was not Americanism at all, that coerced belief was not what the American people needed to stay united. This was not Germany or Russia but the country of Jefferson and Justice Holmes.

The flag worship of the American school and the American nation was brought home to the British public in an episode that, if funny, was also very revealing. For the London makers of ladies' underwear

* "I believe in the United States of America as a Government of the people, by the people, for the people; whose just powers are derived from the consent of the governed; a democracy in a republic; a sovereign Nation of many sovereign States; a perfect union, one and inseparable; established upon those principles of freedom, equality, justice, and humanity for which American patriots sacrificed their lives and fortunes. I therefore believe it is my duty to my country to love it; to support its Constitution; to obey its laws; to respect its flag, and to defend it against all enemies."

who adorned their garments with American flags were innocent of any insulting or even frivolous intention. At the same time, a revue chorus in London was attired in Union Jack handkerchiefs and nothing else—to the public indifference. But the flag, in America, is more than a mere symbol among many others. It is the regimental color of a regiment in which all Americans are enrolled. Its thirteen stripes and forty-eight stars are symbols far better understood than the complicated heraldry of crosses of Saint George, Saint Andrew, and Saint Patrick imposed on each other in a way that only experts understand. It was Lincoln's task to see that the number of stars in the flag was not diminished by eleven during his term of office. It was the discovery that the flag still flew over Fort McHenry, despite the British fleet, that moved Francis Scott Key to write:

> Oh, say, can you see by the dawn's early light,
>   What so proudly we hailed at the twilight's last gleaming;
> Whose broad stripes and bright stars, thro' the perilous fight,
>   O'er the ramparts we watched were so gallantly streaming?

What he wrote in 1814, tens of millions of Americans have since sung or tried to sing. And when Barbara Frietchie in Whittier's poem told-off Stonewall Jackson with:

> "Shoot if you must this old gray head,
>   But spare your country's flag," she said,

she was speaking for all Americans for whom the Stars and Stripes was still their country's flag as it had been, till recently, that of General Jackson.

Thus Americanization by ritual is an important and necessary part of the function of the American school. And because it is best carried out in schools, it matters little that the high school curriculum has been so widened that it no longer means a great deal that this boy or that girl has graduated from it—if we are looking for proof of academic achievement. But graduation from high school is reasonable proof that a great deal has been learned about American ways of life, that lessons in practical politics, in organization, in social ease have been learned that could not have been learned in factory or office.

And if the high school seems to devote too much time and money to social life, penalizing the poor boy or girl more than a theoretically less democratic educational system might do, it is thus early impressing an awkward truth on the boy or girl who is both mediocre and poor. It also penalizes the really able boy or girl who is not kept in good enough intellectual training. And if the main business of the school is, in fact, the Americanization of the children of newcomers, the parents of "old American stock" have a good reason (to add to less good ones) for not sending their children to learn what they know already, at the cost of diminishing their chance of learning what they do not know. If English is native to your children and to their home, it is not merely undemocratic to object to having their progress held up and their accent debased by the tone of a high school largely immigrant in composition.

For the task of an American school in many regions is to teach the American language, to enable it to compete with Spanish, with French, with Yiddish, with Polish, with German, with Swedish. Another task is to give, through the language and the literature of the language, a common vocabulary and a common fund of allusion, fable, and sentiment. With a fluid population this has not been easy. And the countless teachers who have labored, pedantically, formally, with complete and erroneous conviction that there were correct standards, have been heroes as important in the mass as was William McGuffey whose *Eclectic Readers* sold over one hundred and twenty million copies and helped to make the Union. The teachers were heroes because, although English won against all its rivals, it was itself going through important changes, in vocabulary, in grammar, in sound, becoming the new tongue we are beginning to call American. The teachers who stuck by the rules, who worshipped at the New England shrines in Concord, were bound to lose, but their struggle was not pure waste. For the common tongue, hammered out by millions of immigrants, by millions of migrants, would have been poor in vocabulary and structure but for the people Mr. Mencken calls the dominies and who call themselves schoolmen. The creation of general literacy and a common written and spoken tongue, intelligible everywhere except possibly in the deep South, is an achievement as remarkable as the creation of Mandarin Chinese

[1 3 9]

or Low Latin or Hellenistic Greek, and this tongue is certain to be the new *lingua franca* of the world.

The making of American has been mixed-up in English minds with the making of American slang. Slang, as we should know, is one of the great sources of language. French is improved Latin slang. And slang has contributed a good deal to American. It is a generation since Mr. Dooley said that when his countrymen had finished with the English language it would look as if it had been run over by a musical comedy. Since then it has been run over by *Hellzapoppin*. But it is possible, indeed very easy, to overestimate the role of slang. It is more and more the creation of professional artists, "makers." The Hollywood prose masters provide a current and often short-lived jargon; the boys and girls, men and women, who wish to be on the beam or in the groove, may murmur with admiration, "I wish I had said that." And Whistler's classical answer to Wilde is certainly appropriate: "You will, Oscar—you will!" But not for long. Some slang will enter the language; some words will lose their meanings or acquire new ones; syntax will be loosened up. But formal speech as taught in schools will still be very important. The high school English teacher, for all her pedantry, is as much a maker of the American language as Messrs. Runyon and O'Hara. Two streams of language may run roughly parallel, but in time they will merge; they will provide America with many interesting variations, do for American what its dual Germanic and Latin character does for English. That time has not yet come, but it is on the way. And the future character of this truly national tongue is foreshadowed in the drawing by Mr. Peter Arno in which an indignant citizen tells another: "I consider your conduct unethical and lousy."

Most American parents do not want, or are not able, to send their children to anything but public high schools, and the life in such a school is a training in life for America. It may be and often is a training in life *against* Europe. For Europe is the background from which many of the children are reacting and from which they must be delivered if they are to be Americanized. For nearly all immigrants, America is promotion, and this promotion is more clearly felt by their children. The old people may hanker after the old country, but the children—whatever sentimental feelings for their ancestral homes they may have, especially when provoked—are, above all else, anxious to be Americans.

Necessarily something is lost here. The least-common-denominator Americanism of the schools is not a complete substitute for a native culture. What the first-generation American children learn to despise may include elements in their moral diet that are not replaced. A new American whose pride in that promotion involves mere contempt for the habits, what Americans call the "folkways" or "mores," of his parents is not necessarily a good American. So attempts are made to instill pride in the ancestral cultures of the European lands from which the immigrants come. The University of Pittsburgh, located in one of the main melting pots of America, has a set of rooms illustrating the culture of various European countries. In the case of the Greeks, the room may instill adequate pride; in the case of the Scots (if any such need is felt) a shrine of Robert Burns may serve. But, for many of the peasant immigrants, the old country is backward though beloved, while for their children it is merely backward.

Americanization comes not from preservation of Slovak or Italian peasant culture, but from speedy assimilation to "American" culture. And that assimilation may take the form of distinction in anything that the American world obviously values. In the narrow sense of culture, there may even be a temptation to go for those courses that have no immigrant stigma on them. Thus I have been told by an eminent Scandinavian-American that it is difficult to get good students of Scandinavian literature and language at the University of Minnesota, although most of the students have fairly recent Scandinavian connections. They will study French but not Swedish, for "French is not a servant's language." Latin, emblem of functionless "culture," plays something of the same role; it is a symbol of liberation.

Study is not the only way up to Americanization, to acceptation. Sport is another—and one that does the job more dramatically for the newcomers gifted with what it takes to excel in competitive contests, with what is needed to win personal and community and institutional glory.

When Fanny Ellsler, the ballet dancer, came to Boston, her performance was solemnly inspected from the highest motives by Emerson and Margaret Fuller. "The dance began; both sat serenely silent; at last Emerson spoke. 'Margaret,' he said, 'this is poetry.' 'No, Waldo,' replied Margaret; 'it is not poetry, it is religion.'" * And the great football games of today are religious ceremonies in this sense. It is significant that the graduating classes in Muncie High School a generation ago took such mottoes as "Deo duce" and today take mottoes stressing the "Bearcat Spirit," the "Bearcats" being the school basketball team. But a Greek would know where he was at a basketball game uniting boys and girls, parents and civic leaders, in a common passion for competitive achievement. It may be hard on the academic work of the school. It may even slightly annoy a schoolboy, who like Mr. Burton Rascoe combines excellence in gymnastic and music (as the Greeks put it), to find that his views on literature are less interesting to the other sex than his prowess at football. But sport, school sport, college sport, does unite the parents, the children, and the community. And sport is rigorously democratic. The sons of Czechs and Poles can score there, can break through the barriers that stand in the way of the children of "Bohunks" and "Polacks." And although Harvard may secretly rejoice when it can put a winning team on to Soldiers' Field whose names suggest the *Mayflower*, it would rather put on a team that can beat Yale, even though it is not a "Yankee" team, than go down to defeat with the descendants of generations of Brahmins. And in the Middle West, sport is a real means of promotion. The Ohio high school that produced the great Negro runner, Jesse Owens, was prouder of him than if he had made Phi Beta Kappa at Ohio State; and Hitler would have made a less serious mistake if he had snubbed a great American scholar whose race he didn't like than he did by sulking at the Olympic Games when the Herrenvolk were beaten by a Negro. It is a frontier tradition; Lincoln's great strength gave him a prestige that helped him as a lawyer and politician. The great athlete performing for the glory of the school, college, state, or nation, is a less egoistic figure than the great scholar pursuing his own studies with an undemocratic concentration. And the Negroes, whose greatest hero is Joe Louis, not Paul Robeson, are not substantially wrong so far. In American so-

* Barrett Wendell: *A Literary History of America*, p. 301.

ciety as it is, a Negro heavy-weight champion, like a Negro tap-dancer, is a better adjusted figure than a great Negro artist—or America is a less maladjusted society for them. Of course, this will not and should not last. The Irish were rising when their great hero became Governor Al Smith, rather than a successor of John L. Sullivan, the "Boston strong boy." But to get assent to a Negro's *right* to be heavy-weight champion is something—as those will agree who remember the frenzied search round 1910 for a "white hope" to save the heavy-weight championship from the indignity of being held by Jack Johnson. Great Indian athletes like Jim Thorpe, great Negro football heroes like Paul Robeson in his earlier days, the polyglot teams put on the field by the great Swedish coach Knut Rockne for the "Irish" of Notre Dame—these become "All American" figures in a wider and deeper sense than that in which the Yale of Walter Camp understood the term.

The cheer leaders, the new "jongleurs de Notre Dame," the "majorettes," shapely young women more or less involved with musical instruments, the massed cheering sections of the students, the massed yelling sections of the alumni—these are the equivalent of the crowds at the great Hellenic festivals in which barbarians were not allowed to compete. The Rose Bowl, the Cotton Bowl, the other intersectional games—these are instruments of national unity, and the provision of such instruments is no mean duty of colleges and universities. It is a religious exercise of a kind a Greek would have understood, however remote it may be from the university as understood by Abelard or Saint Thomas Aquinas or John Harvard.

The university, as these men understood it, exists all the same and exists to play a great national part, for the level of academic learning in America is perhaps the only branch of American life where the promise of rapid progress upward has been consistently kept. It is not as easy to define the nature of that progress as it is to affirm its existence.

Things have changed a great deal since the ideal of American college education was "Mark Hopkins at one end of a log and a student at the other." Then the college existed to provide a common background for lawyers and doctors and divines; it was small and select, not select in a social or financial sense, but select in that only those who accepted the old intellectual order of things were catered for. It was a decisive moment when President Eliot of Harvard (which had long ceased to concentrate on providing for a "learned ministry") introduced the elective system. The college abandoned any idea of imposing a hierarchy of subjects. The student could select what he wanted from the menu provided; *à la carte* had succeeded *table d'hôte*. But in newer, less secure, less rich institutions than Harvard, the change went farther than that, for not only was the student free to choose from what was offered—he was entitled to complain if the college did not offer what he wanted to learn, or even what he wanted to learn in the sense that it was all he could hope to learn. As more and more students came to college with varying school preparation, as life grew more complex and the techniques of life and business more impressive in their results, the unity of college life disappeared. Boys and girls were no longer taken in hand by a successor of Mark Hopkins and given a few general ethical and philosophical ideas suitable to a world still pretty much agreed on fundamentals. They were visitors to an institution that seemed to have more in common with the Mark Hopkins Hotel in San Francisco than with the Williams College of a century ago; and from the glass-walled bar, "The Top of the Mark," they could see the modern world, the bridges and skyscrapers of San Francisco, and across the Bay the lights of Berkeley where the University of California provides for all tastes from addicts of the Greek theater to the most modern biological and physical techniques.

In this necessary adaptation of the old university ideal to the modern American world, much was lost, or not provided; there was not as yet a common standard of reference for educated men; a mass of information was stored and techniques were imparted in institutes physically associated for historical reasons. But of course, the universities and colleges like the high schools, served other than merely academic ends. *Our Town* illustrates high school mating which would have taken place anyway. *The Miracle of Morgan's Creek* shows a suitor taking cookery so as to be close to his beloved during her high school career, but he was bound to be close to her anyway. But the college movie, play (*The Poor Nut*) and novel rightly illustrates the more important phenomenon of exogamous marriage, of the bringing together boys and girls who otherwise would not meet at all.

Besides all these activities (formally described as extra-curricular) there is, of course, a great deal of first-class academic work done. And in one very important field the American public, if it wills, is given admirable opportunities for learning relevant facts about the modern external world as well as about its own past and present. No charge can be less well founded than that which holds the American school of today up to scorn for its uncritical jingoism. It is no longer true that American history is taught as a simple story of black (George III) vs. white (George Washington). A generation of critical scholarship has borne fruit in an objective and even slightly cynical treatment of the American Revolution and other great crises of American history. If the old simple story is still told and believed, that is not the fault of the schools. And contemporary American life is treated with the same candor. Nothing could be in more striking contrast than the legend of southern life as it is told and retold by politicians and preachers and the grim, courageous, critical studies of the contemporary South that come from the universities, above all from the University of North Carolina.

It is not only American problems that are studied and analyzed with such learning, acuteness, and candor. World problems are, too. There is no country in the world where discussion of the world's affairs is carried on at such a high level as in the United States. (There are also few countries where it is carried on at such a low level, but that is another story.) Serious discussion, in great newspapers and magazines, in forums and on the air, in universities and institutes is incessant. And it is discussion by real experts. Unfortunately, it is often discussion for experts, not for the people. For them, as the *Saturday Evening Post* rightly pointed out, the most complicated subjects in international politics are just another "study subject," the theme of accurate and objective but rather chilly debate by those who like that kind of thing.

And the very success of the school system in Americanizing the American young may result in the killing of natural curiosity. For example, the cult of the Constitution leads to the exclusive identification of a political concept like "liberty" with the American constitutional system. This being so, a Latin-American "republic" with a paper constitution like the American is regarded as "free" while Canada is not. For Canada is part of an "empire" with a monarch at the head of it. Some two-thirds of the American people, accordingly, think that Canada pays taxes to Britain; even in the states bordering on the Dominion, about half the Americans think this! In the same way, the word "republic" has an almost magical significance for the Americans. Plutarch, as Mr. Wells once suggested, had a good deal to do with this; but, whatever the origins of the belief, it is now part of the American credo that only citizens of a republic can be free. And no matter what romantic interest Americans may display in the human side of monarchy, it should never be forgotten that, politically, they regard it as a childish institution. Mark Twain, a very pro-English American, refused for that very reason to write one of his amusing, critical travel books about England. But he did write two books about England, all the same: *The Prince and the Pauper* and *A Connecticut Yankee at the Court of King Arthur.* How deeply anti-monarchical, anti-clerical, anti-traditional, those books are!

And in *Huckleberry Finn,* the traditional American view of royalty as expensive foolishness is admirably set forth in Huck's remark to Nigger Jim: "Sometimes I wish we could hear of a country that's out of kings."

A great many Americans still think like Huck Finn. And it must be remembered that for Americans the great event of their own and of world history was the destruction of the royal power of George III and the establishment of a Constitution guaranteeing to each State "a republican form of government." It is in that light that the modern world is seen by nearly all Americans.

Nothing is more natural and understandable than the American assumption that all modern historical events are either American or unimportant. The Pole who wrote a book on *The Elephant and the Polish Question* was not merely a typical Pole but a typical human being. There are remote academic subjects that we study, and real, living subjects that concern us. "Listen to my bomb story and I'll listen to yours," as they said in London in 1940. Therefore the American conviction that the First World War really began in 1917, and that this one began on December 7th, 1941, is simply an American example of a general illusion. We know that the Chinese were fighting the Japanese long before we were, but we don't *feel* it. We could remember, if we tried, that the Poles were fighting the Germans a little before the British and long before the Russians or the Americans, but we don't feel any urgency to recall it. The Americans who, in March 1944, learned that their countrymen had bombed Berlin for the first time were astonished. The "We" who bombed Berlin in 1943 included Americans psychologically, but the "We" who bombed Tokyo didn't include British either factually or psychologically. This is all part of human nature. The Russians, with little experience of navigating on the high seas, can hardly be expected to appreciate that crossing the English Channel and invading is not quite the same thing as crossing even a wide river. Julius Caesar's Mediterranean sailors, after all, had to learn that the hard way in 55 B.C. Of course this human attitude can be carried to extravagant lengths. A Frenchman might or might not be amused, but would certainly be surprised, to learn from a handout of the National Geographic Society that it was "Decatur's courage [which] paved the way for colony-minded France to annex most of Barbary to her African empire." *

Such an attitude can be very irritating, yet the assumption that world history is part of American history is healthier than any belief that the two are completely separate and that the one is real while the other is merely interesting. It is only when the heads and hearts of the American people are touched that they can be induced to listen to a call from the outer world for leadership. And that leadership will be given only if moral as well as material interests are involved. The only appeal that will be listened to will be the appeal to come over to Macedonia and help.

"It will be no cool process of mere science. . . . The feelings with which we face this new age of right and opportunity sweep across our heartstrings like some air out of God's own presence, where justice and mercy are reconciled and the judge and the brother are one. . . . Men's hearts wait upon us; men's lives hang in the balance; men's hopes call upon us to say what we will do. Who shall live up to the great trust? Who dare fail to try? I summon all honest men,

* *New York Times,* February 13th, 1944.

all patriotic forward-looking men, to my side. God helping me, I will not fail them, if they will but counsel and sustain me." * Till that note is struck again no answer can be expected from the plain people.

But in the meantime, millions of young Americans, serving their country, if not as yet any general cause, are exiled in foreign world for which their training in a sense has unfitted them. For that training was based on the theory that there is an answer available to every question; all you have got to do is to find the right authority, whether the question relates to the technique of football, of spot-welding, or of love. There is a charming optimism in this view, an optimism that, in America, is justified most of the time. It creates a world in which, as a wise American friend of mind said, there are known Plimsoll lines in most fields of conduct. It is a world in which formal good manners and comradeship are both happily cultivated between the sexes. It is true that the hearty camaraderie which is so charming at twenty palls a little at thirty and may give superficial justification for the sour remark of a European critic that "what the American woman suffers from is too much poor-quality attention." It may even justify another view—that American men and American women are better company apart than together, and that the men are better company than the women. But these illusions of solutions attained, in politics and in life, are a tribute to the success with which Amercan life has been made attractive to Americans, to the vast majority of Americans who feel at home in America and are consequently swept away from their moorings in a strange world whose standards they cannot understand and from whose apparent moral and political anarchy they long to escape by going home.

* Woodrow Wilson, *First Inaugural* (1913).

◇◇◇◇◇◇◇◇◇◇◇◇

PART THREE

The American Way in War

*"I will fight it out on this line
if it takes all summer."*
—GENERAL U. S. GRANT, 1864

Most American towns, big and little, are well provided with public statuary. There are the usual frock-coated philanthropists and politicians; there are monuments to record-breaking cows; to long-dead and therefore safely admired Indian chiefs; there is even a monument to the boll-weevil, which by killing the cotton crop forced one southern region into diversified farming. But the typical monument of an American town, north of the Mason and Dixon line and east of the Missouri, is a cast-iron statue to some hero of the Civil War, the most American of American wars. There they stand, with their little French képis over their ears, with their muskets or sabers, products of the main industry of a small New England town that made a corner in the business. In bigger cities generals ride on bronze horses, even generals whose public and private record was far from brilliant are thus honored. And in Washington, city of monuments, there are enough statues to soldiers, more or less distinguished, to make a Prussian paradise.

But there is one American soldier who has few monuments and little popular fame. Nevertheless it is George Brinton McClellan—

[149]

at thirty-four General in Chief of the Union armies, and a year later unemployed, in personal and political disgrace—who is the typical American *successful* soldier; his way of war is the American way of war, and, even if he did not win the Civil War, it was won in his spirit and by his methods.

And that way of war was General Washington's way of war, was the way in which the American continent was conquered and held, the way taught to Americans by their own history, imposed on them by their own needs, and suggested by their own resources. It is a war of lines of communication, of supply, of material. Long before the term "logistics" became fashionable, the science was practiced by the organizers of little expeditions against the Indians, by the leaders of expeditions, peaceful in intent, across the plains to California, down to Santa Fe. *Space* determined the American way in war, space and the means to conquer space. Into empty land the pioneers moved, feeling their way slowly, carefully, timidly if you like. The reckless lost their scalps; the careful, the prudent, the rationally courageous survived and by logistics, by superiority in resources, in tenacity, in numbers. Americans who did not learn these lessons were not much use in the conquest of the West.

For from the beginning of their settlement, the colonists were faced with enemies who, once they had got guns and gunpowder, knew the million square miles of forest better than did the white new-comers. They knew all its possibilities and dangers, its trails, its swamps, its snakes, its poison oak and its poison ivy, its salt licks, its portages on the rivers, its passes in the mountains—knew them as well as a good German staff officer knows the country behind the West Wall. Some of these tribes, above all the Iroquois, were as militarized, were as much an army possessing a state, as modern Prussia or Paraguay or ancient Sparta. They could be fought, they could be conquered, only by patience, prudence, the massing of superior resources, the ignoring of opportunities for brilliant action till the time came. As Frontenac broke the threat of the Iroquois to the existence of New France, so, nearly a century later, General Sullivan cleared upstate New York for the settlement which has given that state Rome and Syracuse and Troy, Cato and Utica, where the Six Nations once ruled like the Spartiates or Chaka's Zulus. But it was not only General Sullivan who learned, for the young George Washington began his military career with the humiliating experience of being forced to surrender *by starvation* to more forest-wise French; and he saw, with his own eyes, the limitations of British military methods when that admirable parade-ground general, Braddock, marched straight ahead into the French and Indian country to death and the practical annihilation of his army. Other British generals have done the same; courage can work wonders, but not all wonders, and the Virginians were not so much won to respect by the courage as to horror or irony at the irrelevance of parade-ground virtues. For Americans, then and now, the battle is *always* the pay-off, to borrow Major Ingersoll's phrase. Victory is the aim, and the elegance of the means is a European irrelevance, recalling the days when war was the sport of kings. To Americans, war is not the sport of kings but the most serious national and personal concern which they like to fight in their own way and which, when they do fight it in their own way, they win.

This, of course, is concealed from Americans as well as from us by schoolboy romanticism. It is far more encouraging to daydreams to think of the West as having been won by a handful of totally reckless scouts and pioneers, hoping for an Indian war rather than fearing it, and ready to plunge into the trackless wilderness at the drop of the hat. There *were* people like that, reckless of their own and their fellows' lives. But they are not heroes to be remembered but horrible examples to be digested and then forgotten. Even the great romantic figures—Daniel Boone, Simon Kenton, even Bridger and Frémont— were heroes because they were *pathfinders,* men who did not get lost, did not venture into trackless places with no knowledge of where they were going. They were pathfinders for the solid, sober, cautious, anxious-to-live pioneers. Without the maps, without the oral or written instructions that those men provided, more parties of western-moving settlers would have suffered the fate of the Donner party: starvation, cannibalism, death, in the High Sierra or, like many less famous victims, on the High Plains or the grassy sea of the prairie. And behind the Boones and Kentons, the Bridgers and Frémonts, were the businessmen, George Washington and Leland Stanford. Matter-of-fact men, some of them rascals; all of them men with a clear head for bookkeeping. They wanted to settle men and women and cattle peacefully; they wanted to do it cheaply; they knew that distance was the enemy, the great weapon of the Indian and of his allies, hunger and thirst. So trails and roads, rivers that would float rafts and canoes and keel boats, salt licks where the cattle could restore their health, malaria-free ground where camps could be made—these were the elements of the problem of opening up the perpetual second front of the West. These provided for, the Indians could be conquered, perhaps without fighting. So the commander of Virginian riflemen under General Washington who had won the name of Mad Anthony Wayne was the general who, under President Washington, carefully prepared to avenge the defeats of his predecessor, defeats caused by bad and inadequate preparation. General Wayne did not rush on the Indians as if they had been British regulars of the old school; he prepared, with unsporting thoroughness, to move, safely and in overwhelming force. Long before he won the Battle of Fallen Timbers, Wayne had won the war and the prize of war, the Ohio country—won it from the Indians and from their British backers in the old French fort of Detroit.

As mad (in the American sense) as Anthony Wayne was that passionate pioneer, Andrew Jackson, favorite hero of his successor in the White House and in the leadership of the Democratic party, Mr. Roosevelt. But when Jackson fought the Cherokees he was as prudent up to the final decisive and morally-testing moment of battle as Wayne or Washington. He was as cautious then, he the duelist and political gambler, as he was ten months later, waiting for the Peninsular veterans of General Pakenham to march up to his breastworks outside New Orleans and be shot down in rows, as if they had been confronting German machine guns and not merely the rifles of well-hidden and practically safe frontiersmen.

The instances could be multiplied almost indefinitely. American history has some equivalents of the charge of the Light Brigade, or of the French cavalry at Reichshofen, or the German cavalry at Mars la Tour. But not many; and even the few there are illustrate the American way in war. Pickett's charge at Gettysburg, the destruction of the "flower of Virginia," is very famous, but it was very futile; it was a gesture regretted by Lee and condemned by Longstreet, that unamiable, overcautious, selfish soldier, more trusted by the rank and file of the Army of Northern Virginia than was either of the great twin brethren of brilliant battle, Lee and Jackson. The real American charge into the deadly breach was exemplified a few months later at Chattanooga when Philip Sheridan led his men racing up the mountain (waving them on, so one tradition has it, with a whisky bottle for a sword) and swept away the army of Braxton Bragg. And that dramatic "battle above the clouds" was a mere finale to a long play whose dénouement had been decided weeks before when the drab figure of General Grant appeared to take over from the brilliant Rosecrans—and Grant got a line of supplies opened into Chattanooga, a line down which poured the endless resources of the North to be launched suddenly, when the issue was beyond all doubt, like an avalanche pouring uphill on the gallant, outnumbered, under-equipped Southern army. Once the way was opened for the fields and factories of the North to supply Chattanooga, the campaign was over. The South could not exploit its victories; it could pick up tricks but not win a rubber. It had defeated Rosecrans, but it could not break that tenacious Virginian serving the North, George Thomas. He was the Rock of Chickamauga on which Grant built. And Thomas, a year later, waited even more patiently than Washington and Wayne while the brilliant thruster, Hood, fought and maneuvered and displayed initiative and fighting spirit. Thomas, indeed, waited so long that the impatient civilian Secretary of War, Stanton, wanted to remove him; but when the due time came, Thomas struck, and on December 15–16, 1864, in the battle of Nashville, he destroyed forever the Southern army in a victory "without a morrow" as complete as Cannae or Sedan. But that victory had been made easy more than a year before, when Thomas had held the railway and river nodal point of Chattanooga. It was a problem in statistics, in organization, in patience, an engineering problem. It is fitting that one of the greatest dams of the Tennessee Valley Authority should bear the name of Chickamauga, the name of one of those battles which decided that for twenty-five hundred miles the Mississippi should "flow unvexed to the sea" through a nation united by arms.

But, as has been said, there is in America, as elsewhere, the legend of campaigns much more like sporting events than these drab accumulations of overwhelming material resources. There are such campaigns. While General Nathan Bedford Forrest did not say that his scheme of war consisted in "getting there fustest with mostest," * some such policy was imposed on the South. They could have force only in terms of time. The North could have force in terms of space which they could command as no one can command time. So Lee was forced to attempt miracles of movement, miracles that, with his inferior resources in men, railways, transport, even food, he did not always work. He asked far too much of his troops, of his staff, of his second-in-command, in the campaign of the Seven Days where he had, facing Jackson and himself, the cautious, the fearful, the egoistic, the neurotic, the beloved and trusted and competent maker and leader of the Army of the Potomac, General McClellan. He asked too much in the concentration before Gettysburg; he did not ask too much when he exploited the fears of Hooker and the unknown trails of the Wilderness, or when in that scrub country he used all the arts of a great defensive general who had been trained as a tamer of the Mississippi, maker of locks and dams, to force General Grant to "fight it out on that line if it took all summer." Grant lost more men in that campaign than there were in Lee's whole army, but he was stronger at the end of it than he was at the beginning. He was strong enough *not* to continue to fight it out on that line, except morally, strong enough to shift his whole army to new bases, supplied by sea, invulnerable to Southern attack, shift it to the position chosen two years before by General McClellan. And from that position he was able to send out Sheridan to destroy the Valley of Virginia as thoroughly and as ruthlessly as the R.A.F. and the American Air Force are destroying the power of movement and of supply of the Reichswehr. Sheridan had to gallop twenty miles to rally his surprised troops, but a defeat at Winchester would have been only a minor inconvenience. A few months later, when Lee's army was desperately lunging south to find food and space to move in, Sheridan by his brilliant improvisation ended the war; but he ended it only a few days sooner than it would have ended anyhow. The decision

* Thanks to the vigilance of *The Baltimore Sun,* I now know better than to disfigure General Forrest's grammar.

that it would end—and end one way—was made when Sherman seized and burned the great railroad center of Atlanta and left Thomas to deal with the Southern army while he marched to the sea, almost unopposed, but breaking the will and the power of the South to resist. This march through Georgia of the young men of Sherman's army was, for them, a kind of picnic. They ran hardly more risk (except from an occasional Scarlett O'Hara) than did the young men of the Luftwaffe in the pleasant early summer of 1940 in the empty skies of France. But Sherman's army had waiting for them, on the coast, the new Northern fleet created out of next to nothing in two or three years—waiting with food and supplies and news and security. They were not like the unfortunate British and German soldiers of Gentleman Johnny Burgoyne marching to a new Saratoga. They were serving not George III and Lord George Germain, but a patient Illinois lawyer, Lincoln, who knew the West; a detestable railway lawyer, Stanton, who knew business; and that unromantic, imperturbable, undignified commander, General Grant.

That fleet itself was a highly rational, functional creation. Its boldest technical innovation in the war was the *Monitor*, the "cheesebox on a raft," the ancestor of the modern heavily armored, turreted gun platform that is the battleship. The Confederate *Virginia* (née *Merrimac*) was a plated man-of-war of the old type, far nearer to Nelson's *Victory* than to a modern battleship. But the real Union navy, created out of nothing, was the utilitarian fleet of gunboats and fast, light-draft cruisers that caught the blockade runners, the equivalent of Coastal Command. That fleet went wherever the ground was a little damp—as Lincoln put it. It learned all the arts of amphibious operations on the high seas and in the great rivers. How many Americans who in the fall of 1943 were anxious over Salerno, for a day or two, remembered Pittsburg Landing, better known as Shiloh? It was an operation of the Salerno type, bloody and bitterly fought but on a greater scale. Admiral Samuel Du Pont (of the great munitions family) off Charleston, Admiral David Porter in the Mississippi—these are not such dramatic figures as that great Catalan-American sailor, Farragut, forcing the mined and fortified approaches of New Orleans or Mobile, having himself tied to his mainmast like a new

Ulysses and giving the famous order, "Damn the torpedoes!" (i.e., mines); but they are all representative officers of a service which, though until 1942 it had never fought a really great sea battle, not only had to its credit a brilliant series of single-ship actions, but also had learned to work with an army over four long and grim years, and had helped to secure for the North the time to turn one of the least armed and most pacific nations of modern times into the greatest military power on the globe. For even more in 1861 than in 1917 or 1941, the United States entered a great war in a state of non-preparation that recalls the inadequacy of Irish military methods when the Danes came, or of Mexican military methods when Cortes came armed with the apparently divine weapons of gunpowder and horses.

Americans have long been accustomed to jest at this repeated state of military nakedness. "God looks after children, drunkards, and the United States." There is a truth in that; space, remoteness, have given a little time to prepare—and the American people needs very little time. Hitherto it has had just enough, provided by accident, distance, or allies.

2

SO WE RETURN to General McClellan, the brilliant product of West Point who had been sent to the Crimea to see how the great European nations made war and who had learned, at least, what not to do. He reported; he secured the adoption of a new saddle (still, I am told, an excellent saddle); and he retired to run great railroads. It was an excellent and typical training. Here were the problems of planning, of personnel management, of technical adaptation, of improvisation, for an American railroad in those days required as much elasticity in making and operating as an army on the march in hostile country. He learned to know the West, the growing, precedent-free, elastic country where anything was possible—if you knew how. It was a world very different from the narrow coastal plain, long settled, thickly peopled; a country where it was natural to try to imitate such brilliant maneuvers, such magnificent achievements of the pre-machine age, as Marlborough's march to the Danube in 1704 or Napoleon's march to the Danube in 1805.

But before he could succumb to or resist the temptation to imitate the pre-railway art of war, he had to get an army. The army of the United States in 1861 when the Civil War broke out was 16,000 strong, scattered in tiny posts all over the Indian country. Few officers (apart from those who had served in the Mexican War) had ever seen a thousand soldiers together. The new armies had to be created out of nothing; they were created. A few years before, McClellan had seen in the Crimea the slow and moderately effective creation of an efficient British army helping the French to besiege Sebastopol. Within six months of taking over the command of the Army of the Potomac (an army whose first martial experience had been Bull Run —a disastrous defeat followed by a humiliating rout), an admirably equipped, well-disciplined, coherent army of one hundred and fifty thousand men was learning how to fight, the hard way, in desperate drawn or lost battles. What was done in the East was being done in the West, too. Yet the political head of the War Department was a most representative Pennsylvania politician of an age when, even more than now, Philadelphia was "corrupt and contented." The military head of the army at the beginning of the war was a venerable, corpulent, almost immovable veteran who had been a brilliant success in the War of 1812 and, as an elderly general, had captured Mexico City fourteen years before. Hardly anybody in the United States had taken military matters seriously except the more energetic members of the tiny corps of professional officers—whose ablest leaders, Lee, Joe Johnston, and Albert Sidney Johnston, had gone over to the other side. Yet there were no breakdowns in supply such as made the British army in the Crimea almost unusable for months. Lincoln can hardly be described as stamping on the ground, but armies sprang out of it all the same and the task of conquering eight hundred thousand square miles was undertaken. Brilliant short-cut plans, straight marches on the Southern capital, raids and flanking maneuvers were attempted, with pretty uniformly disastrous results. The war was fought for four years by accumulating slowly but inexorably every kind of material resource, by laboriously teaching troops the very elements of their trade—the pupils being all ranks of officers as well as men.

The American soldier was as critical as the civilian. He despised a good many of his generals, for pretty good reasons. When Grant obstinately renewed futile attacks, his troops pinned letters to their tunics to their kinsfolk since they knew that many would fall outside the Confederate entrenchments but none would cross them. When "Uncle Billy" Sherman sternly rebuked a plundering soldier, he was told: "You can't expect all the cardinal virtues for thirteen dollars a month."

Behind the front there was profiteering; there was the evasion of military service through the purchase of substitutes who, in turn, often earned more than one bounty by enlisting over and over again —deserting as soon as they could. There was bitter dispute about the higher conduct of the war, complaints that the West was being neglected in favor of an equivalent of the modern "island-hopping" strategy in the East. But by 1865, with an army two million strong, the United States was the greatest military power in the world and one of the most formidable naval powers. Within fifteen years of the end of the war, she had again barely enough troops to keep the Indians in order and was reasonably doubtful of her ability to fight a successful naval war with Chile.*

The Spanish War of 1898 lasted too short a time and the Spaniards were so feeble that nothing more was learned than that the American army was ill and the Navy well prepared to fight. When the

---

* The record of American improvisation in the Civil War is so astonishing that it is with a shock that one realizes its technical limitations. Although there were experiments with very novel weapons like repeating rifles on the Northern side and submarines on the Southern side, there was remarkable conservatism in equipment. When General Sheridan watched the Franco-Prussian War of 1870, he had plenty of critical material provided for him, but he was seeing two armies which, very inferior to his own troops in battle experience and battle sense, were better armed. Both had good breech-loading rifles; the Germans had a good breech-loading field gun and the French a promising ancestor of the machine-gun. American technical originality in the sixties was far below its present level.

next testing time came, many of the lessons of the Civil War had been learned—on paper. But in 1917, the army of little more than one hundred thousand men, short in all modern equipment, tanks, airplanes, and modern artillery, had to be turned—and was turned—in a year or so into an army of millions. It was sent overseas in numbers unprecedented in the history of the world, and those fresh, raw troops broke the heart of the Germans. The very reverses shook the temporary victors. As the Confederate army lived off captured Union stores and then sank into nakedness and weariness as that source failed with the cessation of victories, so the Germans were profoundly depressed by the lavish equipment of the Americans and the Allies they supplied. With resources far beyond the dreams of 1861, the United States of 1917-18 swamped the victorious armies of the Second Reich and broke their spirit.

Today, the same process is under way. The professional leaders of the American army are men trained to work in obscurity and often for basically civilian objects. They learn to make great dams, to build and operate civil projects like the Panama Canal, to organize the unemployed. They enter West Point as the necessary preparation for what, in all probability, will be an obscure and dull life. Their promotion in all the higher ranks depends on the good will of the Senate, which has the right to refuse confirmation of presidential nominations. So the professional soldier learns either to avoid politics like the plague or, in rarer cases, to play that dangerous game. Whether he enters the army at all often depends on a political accident, for the candidates for the entrance examination are nominated by Congressmen, and a would-be soldier whose family is Democratic but who lives in a Republican district is usually out of luck, his military dreams shattered forever—unless, like General Marshall, he has the tenacity to enter from one of the semi-official military schools, in General Marshall's case the Virginia Military Institute. And inside this officer corps recruited from men who won commissions in the last war or entered from VMI or the Citadel of Charleston, the West Pointers, wearing their rings, are an inner caste, cut off from the outside world. They do not even have that training in dealing with civilians that a high British officer gets from his War Office experience, since there are (the political chiefs apart) no high civilian officials in the American War Department; all senior officers get a turn of duty in purely administrative jobs.

And this small, almost anonymous body, serving in widely scattered posts kept up for political reasons where once the threat of Indian war provided real justification, have to deal with the elected representatives of a profoundly unmilitary people that becomes warlike only under great provocation. In peacetime they have to prepare elaborate plans for calling on the immense untapped resources of the United States in a future wartime for which no spiritual preparation can be made. They know that they can never be ready for war; that they must always have time given them that they may use space and the resources of space. They know, too, that their countrymen, brought up like all peoples to believe in a gilded version of their own history, forget that all American wars have, like this one, begun with disasters, not victories. They know that their countrymen are temperamental and versatile, easily bored with theory and all of them having to be shown, not simply told.

The American officer, then, must think in terms of material resources, existing but not organized in peacetime and taking much time and thought and experiment by trial and error to make available in wartime. He finds that his best peacetime plans are inadequate for one basic reason: that *any* plan which in peacetime really tried to draw adequately on American resources would cause its author to be written off as a madman; and in wartime, it would prove to have been inadequate, pessimistic, not allowing enough for the practically limitless resources of the American people—limitless once the American people get ready to let them be used. And only war can get them ready for that. The American soldiers can draw, then, but not before, on an experience in economic improvisation and in technical adaptation which no other country can equal. They can draw, too, on a healthily unprofessional attitude. Men will think, with their civilian and very unmilitary ways of doing things, of new and efficient ways of doing military things. They will build air fields in a week and ford rivers under fire in tractors and bulldozers as part of their new day's work—all the more efficiently that it was not their old day's work. So they used and made and unmade railways in the Civil War, the only modern war until 1914. They improvised railway bridges like that "beanpole and cornstalk" bridge that was built in nine days over Potomac Run and took the rail traffic of an army. So they created the great rail and shipping organization in France in 1918 which would have enabled Foch, in 1919, to deliver that "blow that cannot be parried" of which he had dreamed for forty years and which the Americans gave him the means to deliver. But, like the Negro playing possum in the American story, the Germans surrendered—"Don't shoot, Colonel, I'll come down!"

Wars are not won by generals or by plans alone; they are won by men. And the tradition of the American soldier is a practical one—almost overhumorously practical. He has never had much use or perhaps any use for the virtues of the parade ground. When the victorious Northern armies paraded through the streets of the long-beleaguered city of Washington in 1865, the spectators saw, with a natural special affection, the much enduring Army of the Potomac, veterans of so many unsuccessful, bloody, exhausting campaigns fought over the short hundred miles between Washington and Richmond. These were their own men, finally victorious. But the real curiosity was Sherman's western army. They had not driven to and fro through the Virginia Wilderness or bogged in the swamps of the James River. They had fought and marched and fought and marched down the Mississippi, across Tennessee, "from Atlanta to the sea" and up to the rear of Lee's army. And what the spectators saw was an army of boys—not boys in the modern American sense, i.e., men just short of middle age, but boys in their teens and young men in their early twenties. Grant's army was hardly more dressy than its shabby Commander, but Sherman's army loping along, with open necks and hardly any standard equipment, hardened and lithe, confident and brash, this was an American army, formidable, enterprising, humane, and ribald. Nothing could have been less like the armies of Europe than that, and the world was not to see a comparable sight again till the (British) Eighth Army emerged from the desert, clad as its fancy and its resources dictated, living by its own battle-learned discipline, and—if any of the Americans in Tunis had had the necessary historical imagination to see it—spiritual descendant of the American armies that in four years had fought through from the great central valley to the Atlantic coast.

But the American troops in Tunis were like the American troops in any war, needing to learn, ready to learn—after the need had been brought home to them. As Sheridan was told in 1870 by a philosophical Prussian general who saw his troops running away under murderous French fire, all troops "need to be a little shooted." So it was in 1776 and 1812 and 1861 and 1918. But the adjustment will be made, has been made, though in an American way. The heirs of Morgan's riflemen cannot be turned into the equivalent of the Brigade of Guards—at any rate not without great risk of losing what Morgan's riflemen had, which the Guards found was plenty. The American who, in peacetime, is a national figure if he is ready to walk a mile (for anything but a Camel) is, in wartime, fond of riding to the front in a jeep. But it was already said of eighteenth-century Virginia that its poor people would walk five miles to steal a horse to ride one. In a friendly country like the United States, it is impossible to breed soldiers who will automatically forget that an officer is a human being. And in a ribald and irreverent country, it is hard to get officers to insist, with British self-confidence, on their superiority to human weakness. There must be more give-and-take, more ignoring of unessentials, more confidence that in the hour of battle human virtues and common sense will do as much as automatic discipline of the old eighteenth-century type as exemplified at Bunker's Hill and New Orleans.

A country has the kind of army its total ethos, its institutions, resources, habits of peaceful life, make possible to it. The American army is the army of a country which is law-respecting without being law-abiding. It is the army of a country which, having lavish natural wealth provided for it and lavish artificial wealth created by its own efforts, is extravagant and wasteful. It is the army of a country in which melodramatic pessimism is often on the surface but below it is the permanent optimism of a people that has licked a more formidable enemy than Germany or Japan, primitive North America. It is the army of a country whose national motto has been "root, hog, or die." When convinced that death is the alternative, the hog roots. It is the army of an untidy country which has neither the time, the temperament, nor the need for economy. It is the army of a country in which great economic power is often piled up for sudden use; a final decisive military blow is merely a special variety of "corner." It is the army of a country of gamblers who are more or less phlegmatic in taking and calculating their losses, but who feel with all their instincts that they can never go wrong over a reasonable period of time in refusing to sell America short.

So the American way of war is bound to be like the American way of life. It is bound to be mechanized like the American farm and kitchen (the farms and kitchens of a lazy people who want washing machines and bulldozers to do the job for them). It is the army of a nation of colossal business enterprises, often wastefully run in detail, but winning by their mere scale and by their ability to wait until that scale tells. It is the army of a country where less attention is paid than in any other society to formal dignity, either of persons or of occupations, where results count, where being a good loser is not thought nearly so important as being a winner, good or bad. It is the country where you try anything once, *especially* if it has not been tried before. It is a country that naturally infuriates the Germans with their pedantry and their pathological conception of "honor." It is a country that irritates the English with their passion for surface fidelity to tradition and good form. It is the country of such gadget-minded originals as Franklin and Ford. It is a country whose navy, fighting its first great battles a century and a half after it could boast of Paul Jones, recovered from a great initial disaster and taught the heirs of Togo with what speed the heirs of Decatur and Farragut could back out of their corners, fighting. The Coral Sea, Midway, these are dates for the world to remember along with the new Thermopylae of the Marines at Wake Island or the new Bloody Angle of Tarawa. It is a country—and so an army—used to long periods of incubation of great railroads and great victories. It is the army of a people that took a long time to get from the Atlantic to the Pacific and that found the French and the Spaniards and the Russians before them. But they got there and stayed. The two hundred and fifty years from Virginia to California, like the four years from Washington to Richmond, must be remembered by us—and the Germans. That General Washington, after six years of barely holding his own, combined with the French fleet to capture a British army as easily as taking a rabbit in a snare—that is to be remembered too, for it was a matter not of fighting but of careful timing, of logistics.

That typical western soldier and adventurer, Sam Houston, waiting patiently until the Mexicans had rushed on to deliver themselves into his hands at San Jacinto—that is to be remembered. It is not Custer foolhardy and dramatic with his long hair and his beard who is the typical Indian fighter, but great soldiers like Sherman and Sheridan planning from St. Louis or Chicago the supplying of frontier posts, the concentration of adequate force. The Indian chiefs Joseph and Rain-in-the-Face were often artists in war at least on a level with Rommel. But to the Americans war is a business, not an art; they are not interested in moral victories, but in victory. No great corporation ever successfully excused itself on moral grounds to its stockholders for being in the red; the United States is a great, a very great, corporation whose stockholders expect (with all their history to justify the expectation) that it will be in the black. Other countries, less fortunate in position and resources, more burdened with feudal and gentlemanly traditions, richer in national reverence and discipline, can and must wage war in a very different spirit. But look again at the cast-iron soldier of the Civil War memorial. A few years before, he was a civilian in an overwhelmingly civil society; a few years later he was a civilian again in a society as civilian as ever, a society in which it was possible to live for many years without ever seeing a professional soldier at all, in which 25,000 soldiers, mainly in the Indian country, were invisible among fifty million people minding their own business. Such a nation cannot "get there fustest with mostest." It must wait and plan till it can get there with mostest. This recipe has never yet failed, and Berlin and Tokyo realize, belatedly, that it is not going to fail this time—that in a war of machines it is the height of imprudence to have provoked the great makers and users of machines and, in a war of passions, to have awakened, slowly but more and more effectively, the passions of a people who hitherto have fought only one war with all their strength (and that, a civil war), but who can be induced by their enemies, not by their friends, to devote to the task of making the world tolerable for the United States that tenacity, ingenuity, and power of rational calculation which decided between 1861 and 1865 that there should be a

United States which would twice crush the hopes of a nation of military professionals, to whom war is an art and a science, to be lovingly cultivated in peace and practised in war. For Americans, war is almost all of the time a nuisance, and military skill a luxury like Mah-Jongg. But when the issue is brought home to them, war becomes as important, for the necessary period, as business or sport. And it is hard to decide which is likely to be the more ominous for the Axis— an American decision that this war is sport, or that it is business.

Conclusion

"Here between the hither and the further shore
While time is withdrawn, consider the future
And the past with an equal mind."
—T. S. Eliot

The American problem is the problem of all free peoples in the modern world. It is the problem of how to extend some of the loyalty, the vigilance, the energy of national life to the world in which the national society has to live and whose peace, order, and development are more and more essential conditions of the good life of all national societies, of British, Russian, and American.

A generation ago, this problem seemed much easier of solution than it can seem today. It was then possible to believe that the kind of devotion and energy which the nation-state had evoked could be transferred, without serious loss in transit, to a new world community, whether that world community was interpreted in terms of class, race, religion, or the whole mass of men of good will. But we have seen the failure of all such simple solutions; the failure of the Second and the Third Internationals; of the international authority of the Catholic Church; of the international conspiracy of the Third Reich. Only a small number of men and women in any society are prepared to do for *any* international body what most men and women do, without hesitation, for their national society. Millions of Catholics fight against millions of Catholics; hundreds of thousands of Germans recruited from Communist sections of the German population fight to the death against Russian soldiers stirred to heroic resistance by the memory of old Russian wars. How comparatively few in numbers and energy are the Quislings who serve the Third Reich or the Communist zealots who serve the Third International!

In this there is nothing to surprise us. What should surprise us is the success with which tens of millions of men have been led to feel a common tie that holds them to the point of death. The great nation-state is the phenomenon to be explained, not the failure of that nation-state to merge in a world community. And every nation-state is the result of a long historical process that has marked its people profoundly, in the course of which that people has come into being, united within itself and to some degree necessarily insulated against the outside world. The American people has been so made in a historical experience whose outlines I have tried to describe. Necessarily that historical experience has created the state of mind that I have called "natural isolationism." A nation, like an individual, cannot do everything at once; it cannot care deeply for everything at once, or learn all habits at the same time. It must practice a certain avarice of the emotions, an economy of political and social techniques.

The critical period in the life of a national society comes when it has to learn new habits, acquire new emotional attitudes, possibly unlearn some old lessons, forget some old and once useful habits. Such necessary change is painful for an individual and for a people. The cost of the necessary adaptation is very great. It means personal risk, personal discomfort, personal stock-taking. It means, at the present moment, exile for millions of Americans just when they were beginning to be completely at home in their own country. They do not like it. Who would? Two thousand years ago, Virgil, the poet of a comparable crisis, asked:

> "At nos hinc alii sitientis ibimus Afros,
> pars Scythiam et rapidem veniemus Oaxen
> et penitus toto divisos orbe Britannos,
> en umquam patrios longo post tempore finis,
> pauperis et tuguri congestum caespite culmen
> post aliquot, mea regna videns, mirabor aristas?"

The American soldier, you see, is, like Meliboeus, asking himself why he has to go off to Africa and Australia and endure life among the stand-offish Britons. He wants to know how soon he can hope to get back from England or the Solomons to Iowa or Indiana or New York and see the corn again—whether that corn be real or a metaphor for a tenement in the Bronx. He knows—and often feels —what he is fighting *against* (much more clearly in the case of Japan than in the case of Germany). He knows much less and feels much less what he is fighting *for*; the American way of life does not seem to him to be in much danger. In this he is like other people. The English people did not wake up till the very last moment of most urgent danger; other peoples did not wake up, in time, at all. No nation has so far really asked itself or asked its leaders what Lincoln in 1858 asked his audience:

"If we would first know where we are and whither we are tending, we could better judge what to do and how to do it. . . . 'A house divided against itself cannot stand.' I believe this government cannot endure permanently half slave and half free. I do not expect the Union to be dissolved; I do not expect the house to fall; but I do expect it will cease to be divided. It will become all one thing, or all the other."

Lincoln was speaking against a kind of internal isolationism, against a belief that a great internal cleavage, tolerable, practically if not morally, in an earlier and far less integrated stage in American history, could continue to be tolerable when railways had brought two different societies into close, competitive neighborhood and had accelerated the growth of two very different societies. The consequence of failure to face the problem of the house divided was the Civil War—a crude and expensive way of settling a problem that could *perhaps* have been settled otherwise. Historical analogies, though always dangerous, are often valuable, too, and from Lincoln we can at least learn the need for patience and the need for candor, the need for doing what can be done and for not letting all possible good things be the enemy of realizing one good.

The house must cease to be divided if we are to prevent one of the ice ages of history from coming upon us. But it will have to be a house of many mansions, not an enormous room where bored and frightful prisoners regret the varied life they have known.

The American problem is the British problem, the French problem, the Polish problem: the reconciliation of real national autonomy, of real national tradition, with the needs of a new world society. There is no hope at all in creating a world society whose unity is to be bought at the cost of sacrificing what the nations (the only communities that now exist) have painfully learned about themselves. Each nation will have its own handicaps to overcome, but this is given by the nature of the case. The American people can contribute to the world community only as Americans. As Americans they have much to give, materially and spiritually: a well-founded optimism about their own possibilities; a well-founded belief that some of the problems of unity in the absolute essentials, combined with diversity in all departments of life where diversity is possible, have been solved in the American historical experience. The problem set us and all peoples by the technological unification of the world is extremely difficult. It will be hard to solve, at best, and it may easily be made insoluble by pretense that its basic difficulty either does not exist or can easily be got round— the difficulty of creating an effective sense of common duty and common interest among the separate and quite different peoples of the world. That separateness, that difference, need not be insuperable obstacles if they are first allowed for and their origins understood. It is, I have been told, one of the most formidable of Chinese imprecations to wish that your enemy lived "in interesting times." We live in very interesting times; times not to be made better by any simple formula. Understanding each other is not enough, but it is an indispensable beginning.

A NOTE ON THE TYPE

The text of this book is set on the Linotype in Fairfield, the first type-face from the hand of the distinguished American artist and engraver Rudolph Ruzicka. In its structure Fairfield displays the sober and sane qualities of a master craftsman whose talent has long been dedicated to clarity. It is this trait that accounts for the trim grace and virility, the spirited design and sensitive balance of this original type face.

Rudolph Ruzicka—who was born in Bohemia in 1883 and came to America in 1894—set up his own shop devoted to wood-engraving and printing in New York in 1913, after a varied career as a wood-engraver, in photoengraving and bank-note printing plants, as art-director and free-lance artist. He now lives and works at his home and studio in Dobbs Ferry, New York. He has designed and illustrated many books and has created a considerable list of individual prints—wood-engravings, line-engravings on copper, aquatints. W. A. Dwiggins wrote recently: "Until you see the things themselves you have no sense of the artist behind them. His outstanding quality, as artist and person, is *sanity*. Complete esthetic equipment, all managed by good sound judgment about ways and means, aims and purposes, utilities and 'functions'— and all this level-headed balance-mechanism added to the lively mental state that makes an artist an artist. Fortunate equipment in a disordered world. . . ."

COMPOSED, PRINTED, AND BOUND BY
H. WOLFF, NEW YORK